T3-BWP-289

THE LEGAL EDGE

THE LEGAL EDGE

EDGE

FOR HOMEOWNERS, BUYERS & RENTERS

MICHEL JAMES BRYANT, ESQ.

RENAISSANCE BOOKS

Los Angeles

Grateful acknowledgment is made to the California Association of Realtors® for the following forms: Real Estate Transfer Disclosure Statement, Residential Purchase Agreement (and Receipt for Deposit), and Exclusive Authorization and Right to Sell. Reprinted with permission, California Association of Realtors®. Endorsement not implied.

Library of Congress Catalog Card Number: 99–62271
ISBN: 1–58063–066–9

10 9 8 7 6 5 4 3 2 1

Design by Lisa-Theresa Lenthall
Typesetting by James Tran

Distributed by St. Martin's Press
Manufactured in the United States of America

First Edition

To Mom and Dad, you left too soon.

ACKNOWLEDGMENTS

The support of so many made this book possible. The crew at Renaissance; Mike Dougherty and company for their zealous publicity; Lisa Lenthall—thanks for sharing my vision; and most of all to Richard F.X. O'Connor, my editor, who knew when to criticize, when to critique, and when to give in.

Thanks to Alan Frio, Mike Green, Jon Lafayette, Larry Klein, and especially Scott Brown for their kind words. That goes for Pamela Wallace and Ralph Nader too, for taking time away from Academy Award winning writing and Consumer Watchdogging, respectively. To Inge Tucker and Placer Title Company for filling in the blanks.

Finally, to my friends and family who have always been there with support. Special gratitude to Hugh McChord, my TV partner, for his creative stimulus. To Chris Mabe for the tremendous contribution most will never see. To Val for being here when she was far away. To Lisa for her warmth and encouragement. And, most deservedly, my appreciation to the people who have written to ask me about the troubles that make their lives . . . and mine, very interesting.

CONTENTS

LIST OF FORMS

LANDLORD-TENANT SAMPLE FORMS

HOMEOWNER SAMPLE FORMS

FOREWORD

Congratulations! You are well on your way towards gaining "The Legal Edge." You have now done the hard part, you've found a copy of this well-written book. All that's left is the enjoyable part . . . reading it. In America, we live in a representative democracy. A democracy is a government of the people. A representative democracy is a system where the government is run by representatives of the people, rather than by the people themselves. It wouldn't be practical to have a system of government where everyone in America was consulted before any law was passed, any government program was created, or any law was enforced. We, therefore, delegate much of the task of running our government to those we elect to represent us.

Because so much of the task of running our government is delegated to others, many Americans fail to make the effort to understand how our government works. And those of us actually wanting to know more often don't know where to turn for information about our three branches of government—especially when we have questions as to how our judicial system operates.

When I think back to my high school and undergraduate days, the schools I went to did a pretty good job of educating students about the executive and legislative branches of government, but I can't recall spending more than a day or two studying the judicial branch of government. After graduation, knowledge of our legal rights is even harder to come by for most Americans. In fact, most Americans "know" more about our legal system from reading John Grisham books and watching *Ally McBeal* than from any formal education.

Finding legal help has never been more important. Fifty-two percent of all Americans are involved in legal battles of one kind or another right now! This year, you are more likely to spend time in a courtroom than a hospital room. The American Bar

Association reports that 180 lawsuits are filed every minute in this country, and that the average American will need legal help about five times in the next twelve months.

These statistics make it obvious there is a tremendous need in our country for someone to provide accurate, easily understandable legal information. I am thankful that Michel James Bryant has recognized this need. In this important book (and in his syndicated television news pieces) Michel does a tremendous job of providing easily understandable answers to questions you previously didn't even know enough to ask. Best of all, Michel has that rare ability to make a potentially dry topic truly enjoyable.

With this book, the attorney and broadcaster has attacked a topic we all need to understand. Who hasn't had trouble with an unreasonable landlord? Or been confused by the drama involved in the home buying process? We rent. We buy. We move. And then we do it all over again. Now you can do it with the kind of information you need to stay out of legal trouble or take the upper hand if a dispute breaks out. You can only hope the other guy doesn't have this book.

Again, I congratulate you on finding this book. You will enjoy reading it, and the information you glean from it will truly give you "The Legal Edge."

Scott Edmondson Brown
president, National Association of
Trial Lawyer Executives

INTRODUCTION

The law. Charles Dickens was right. "The law is a ass." Or, at least, it can be a pain in that bodily region. Unfortunately, this truth alone will not get you through the legal battles that move in with you where you live. This book will.

Landlord-tenant fights and homeowner battles account for more legal disputes and clogged court calendars than any other consumer problem today. The idea to write this book, came after tons of letters and lots of calls from viewers who watch "The Legal Edge" consumer news feature now seen on television stations throughout the country, letters such as:

> Dear Mr. Bryant:
> Can you give me the legal edge? Neighbor kids are rollerblading on my driveway and I'm afraid they might get hurt and sue me. Can I throw the little brats off my property?
>> V.J.

Or this letter:

> Dear Legal Edge:
> My landlord is an idiot! But she still knows more about the law than I do. Please help me understand my rights.
>> K.P.

Sometimes the questions are silly. Most often serious. By explaining the law that controls Home Sweet Home and by providing practical solutions, this book answers the questions all of us have faced or hope to avoid. Most legal reference books are filled with "the law." That's a good start. But, the law alone is not very helpful without knowing how to make the law work for you.

This book is about helping you help yourself. The American Bar Association estimates more than 100 million people in this country can't get the legal information they need. Even if you can afford professional legal help, you may be tossed into a world that seems foreign and confusing because legal professionals sometimes speak a different language. Consider this book your personal translation guide to help clear the legal haze.

That doesn't mean, by reading this book, I can guarantee you a lawyerless lifetime free of legal trouble. But what you will get is a good basic understanding of the system as it affects the place you call home. More importantly, you'll learn how to prevent or resolve legal problems before you need an attorney or the courts. As part of that process, included throughout, are samples of legal forms like those used in landlord-tenant disputes, small claims court, and in buying or selling a home.

This is not a how-to-sue-somebody book. There are already too many lawsuits in this country, most of them filed by people whining about a problem that could have been prevented. I have represented the whiners. I have also represented the defendants, who proclaim their innocence right up to the point when the jury finds them at fault and whacks them with a large judgment. Much of my work could be avoided if the folks fighting were better armed with a little knowledge and reasonableness.

You may notice a bit of irreverence in the way I describe certain situations, problems, or solutions. I mean no disrespect. The law is a part of life we can't shake, but that doesn't mean we have to be bored to tears while learning about the law and how to make it work in our lives. If a little humor helps make a point or rule more memorable, great. Also, I use the pronouns "he" and "she" in the generic humankind sense and will alternate between the two.

Does this book contain legal advice? No. I am a licensed practicing California attorney, (they call it "practicing law" because some never get it completely right), and it's against the law for me to give legal advice in any state where I'm not licensed. So, because I have a fear of small cramped spaces and guys named "Bubba," this book does not contain legal advice. This book contains legal information.

I hope this information will help you deal with life at home. Those trees the neighbor lets grow into your yard, the potential problems with guests in your apartment, what you do and don't have to tell someone buying your home, and how to get your ex-landlord to cough up the deposit money you deserve. Most of all, this book is supposed to make you think. I know, that isn't a big selling point. But, if thinking can save you money, time, and major hassles, then it will be worth the effort. So here's the knowledge, you supply the reasonableness. The goal is to get the legal edge.

Dear Mr. Bryant:

When I watch you on TV, I often change channels. The reasons that I change channels are as follows:

You do not impress me as a dignified lawyer when you rely so much on theatrical props, climb walls, run down streets, climb ropes, spray with water hoses, climb chandeliers, and all the other (typical unruly child) antics which you perform while allegedly providing expert legal information. Your informal (sleazy) dress, straggly beard, permanent wave and length of your hair are not appropriate for a television program legal expert. You look like a beatnik beachcomber down on his luck. Your physical antics remind one of Cheeta, the little chimpanzee in the old Johnny Weissmuller Tarzan movies. You also need a better writer.

W.W.

Dear W.W.:

Thanks for watching.

M.J.B.

I

DO YOU NEED THE LEGAL SYSTEM?

The System. It has an ominous ring to it. Visions of subpoenas served at embarrassing moments, cranky judges yelling at you, and tons of money spent for things you don't understand and can't play with. Would you like to avoid the system? Read on.

Whether renting, leasing, or buying your home, there will come a time when you feel you've been screwed. Somebody done you wrong and you won't stand for it. You want things fixed right now! Your first reaction may be to run to court or to find a lawyer. Well, not so fast. You need to take a breath and think about the problem—think about the time, money, and effort needed to fix things. It's very likely you can get what you need without the court or expensive legal help. Repeat after me: "Court is my last resort. Court is my last resort. Court is my— hey, look at that girl across the street—oh sorry, got sidetracked. Court is my *last* resort."

1

BEFORE YOU ASK THE JUDGE

NEGOTIATE BEFORE YOU LITIGATE

George is renting an apartment. His friend Steve comes over all the time and parks his motorcycle in one of the parking spaces marked "visitor." The landlord learns of this and George gets a note reminding him that motorcycles are not to be parked on the apartment complex property. George is not happy. George doesn't like the landlord anyway and it's a stupid rule so he never even tells Steve not to park his hog where Steve has been parking his hog. The motorcycle gets hauled away and now Steve is all over George to fork over the towing and storage fees he had to pay the city. George is not happy.

Oh sure, Steve could sue George claiming it was George's fault the bike got towed away. George could sue his landlord claiming that he, as a tenant, had the right to let visitors park where Steve parked. And the landlord could ask the court to kick George out of his apartment for breaking the rules. This is exactly the kind of situation in which negotiation beats litigation.

No matter who is right, it will take a lot more time, energy, and money to get a judge to decide the case than to meet face to face and work things out. Maybe the landlord could have been clearer about the consequences of Steve continuing to park his motorcycle where he did. Maybe George should have followed the rules and told Steve not to park where he did. Maybe Steve could have opened his eyes and read the "No Motorcycles" sign. Maybe this example is getting so long and drawn out that you've got a headache.

You get the picture. Take the time to talk to the other guy *before* you ask the court for help. Even if all fails, you've lost nothing but a little time, and the judge will respect your effort to make things right before bugging him with the problem.

- Decide how much time, effort, and money you can afford to invest in any dispute.

- Make the effort to talk, face to face, to the other side before asking the court or counsel for help.

KNOW WHAT YOU'RE TALKING ABOUT

The best negotiator in the world will fail if he or she doesn't know what the heck he or she is talking about. You need to be armed with info before you try to negotiate any resolution. Your weapons will include a basic understanding of the rules or laws and all the facts needed to explain why you think you should get what you want.

Let's see . . . where can you find the rules that apply to situations involving your home? Hmm . . . well, what do you know? You're holding the very information you need. In this book is the law that controls renting, leasing, and home ownership problems. Use the table of contents or the index to find the area of law you need and then figure out how that law works with the facts of your particular dispute.

A simple example: You're fighting with the landlord over the return of your security deposit. You look up "security deposits" in the index and learn that the landlord must give you a written list of any deductions he makes from your deposit. If you didn't get a list when he sent back only half of your money, you now know the rule that will help you negotiate the dispute. "Mr. Landlord, the law says you are supposed to give me a list of any deductions. You didn't do that. Before I ask the court to help settle this, I would like you to send me the list required by law." Nyah, nyah, nyah. (The last is said silently to yourself.)

The second half of your negotiation arsenal is factual. You need to know all the important facts, not just the ones you like. In our security deposit example, you better have evidence of the physical condition of the place you rent. No proof of how nice you left the home, no refund. That proof may be in the form of pictures, checklists, witness testimony, or letters between you and the landlord. You may not need all of this at the negotiation stage, but having it early and knowing you can use it in court if necessary will make you more confident and better able to handle accusations hurled at you by the landlord, real estate agent, banker, or maintenance man in your face-to-face meeting.

- Learn the rules that apply to your situation.

- Don't play favorites with the facts, know all important details, even if they don't help your case.

- Have the proof to back up the facts and your arguments in any negotiation.

IT'S KIND OF LIKE GOING TO COURT: ARBITRATION AND MEDIATION

You've been reasonable. You've tried talking to the other guy. You've tried sending a well-thought-out professional sounding letter. And you've been ignored. Can I go to court now, Mike? Can I, huh? Can I? Hold on little fella, that may not be your best next step. Start thinking about alternatives to court: arbitration or mediation.

The arbitration and mediation processes have become very popular ways to avoid court and still get professional help settling landlord-tenant and homeowner disputes. First, arbitration. It's like a mini-trial where each side makes its arguments and presents witnesses and evidence to a neutral third person, sometimes an attorney or retired judge. This person is the arbitrator. Once the arbitrator has heard the arguments from both sides, a decision is made. Sometimes that decision is final, (check your lease, rental agreement, or homeowner contracts to see if they include an agreement for "binding" arbitration), and sometimes you are allowed to go on to court if nobody can live with the arbitrator's ruling.

You've also got your mediation. No, not meditation—mediation. Both processes may make you think, but mediation involves more talking, sometimes cursing, and wearing nicer clothes. The best way to describe mediation is to explain how it is different from arbitration. A mediator is a person paid by both sides to reach a compromise. Nobody wins, nobody loses, nobody makes a final decision as in arbitration. The mediator simply works back and forth between the parties, pointing out the weaknesses and strengths of each side's arguments. At some point, the mediator convinces the combatants to meet somewhere in the middle. Mediation is usually successful when both sides walk away feeling like losers. Unlike arbitration, there is no chance to go to court after mediation. The whole idea is to settle the case and when the parties agree to the mediator's proposal, the case is truly over.

Negotiation, arbitration, mediation. All are great ways to save time, money, and emotional energy. But there are times, especially when you face the more complex and costly problems caused by home ownership, that you need to jump into the legal system.

Perhaps even hire a lawyer. If the problem can't be taken care of through negotiation, arbitration, or mediation, then you better learn more about that system and the players you rely on to protect your rights. Read on.

- Check for a clause in your agreement requiring you to use arbitration or mediation.

- Find out the cost of the arbitration or mediation process.

- Make sure you participate in choosing the arbitrator or mediator, then ask friends, family members, or professionals for suggestions.

- Make sure the arbitrator or mediator has experience handling homeowner or landlord-tenant disputes.

II

WELCOME TO THE JUNGLE— YOU'RE IN THE SYSTEM

It's dark. It's creepy. You hear sounds you've never heard before. "Your Honor, Mr. Tenant failed to respond to my subpoena *duces tecum.*" "Judge, this is a basic unlawful detainer action. This Court is being asked to find that my client, the home seller, complied with all state and federal disclosure laws and the buyer assumed the risk." You're tempted to scream, *"Would somebody please speak English?!"*

Oh, it's English all right. In a secret society kind of way. The system is full of special language, special rules, and folks who have been at it so long they no longer use regular speak. Don't let that frighten you. Don't be intimidated by a few fancy words or the suits from which they come.

The key to success in court, any court, is knowing when you are in over your head. Do you need a lawyer? What can you do on your own without screwing things up? At the point you become uncomfortable—you know, just before throwing up—you better get help. The following will either give you comfort or make it easy to tell when you should run like the wind to your favorite attorney.

2

KNOWING THE NUTS AND BOLTS

DO I NEED A LAWYER?

The first question to ask yourself is, "How much money is involved in the fight?" Do you hire an attorney at $150 an hour to win a $500 lawsuit over a rent deposit? (If your answer is "yes," please e-mail me immediately at rucrazy.com.) Do you do your own paperwork when selling a $125,000 home? The answer to this second example is also "no" but you wouldn't believe the number of folks who play Perry Mason with big dollar home sales. And they get into big dollar trouble too. Maybe that's because, when imitating Perry, they forget he was a criminal attorney, not a real estate lawyer.

Second question. How far do you intend to take the battle? We all have a point at which we say, "uncle," "forget it," "it's not worth my time." If all you hope to do is get the other guy's attention or maybe ten cents for each of your lost dollars, you can probably handle the problem yourself. A letter to the landlord about the appliance you paid to fix, a fight with the plumber over his bill, or a demand that your neighbor pay for the fence his dog chewed up—you're not going anywhere but small claims court for these problems.

It kinda looks like these two questions lead to the same conclusion. Big Money/Big Problem— Get Lawyer, Small Money/Small Problem—Don't Get Lawyer. It's just that simple. Especially in the world of renters and homeowners where you can easily figure out your potential loss, the time you might need to fight, and whether there's a potential gain even if you win.

- Figure out how much money is at stake in the dispute.

- Decide how hard you intend to fight and how far you plan to go to get what you want.

I'M JUST A RENTER—WHO CAN HELP ME?

Unless you're renting Trump Tower and The Donald has refused to install the hot tub he promised—you know, the one in the shape of his ex-wives—you are not likely to be justified hiring a lawyer for most rental disputes. You do have other options.

Have you called the local law school? As a former "legal advisor" for my law school, I can tell you that there are plenty of young brains out there dying to help fix your problem—for free! Of course, we were, and most law school advisors are, first- or second-year students with little more than good intentions and lots of big books. But this is a great resource for renters. You can get help writing letters to landlords, learn whether you should withhold rent, make a repair and deduct the cost from your rent, or get the housing authority to check out the dump you are forced to call "home."

Remember though, these are not lawyers, so ask lots of questions and talk to the faculty advisor if you feel uncomfortable about the help you're getting. Oops, that reminds me, I left that lady on hold. . . .

How about the state or local bar associations? Most have referral services that will get you to an attorney, even if it's for just a few minutes of free time. These associations often have regular "people's court" seminars where you can talk to attorneys about general legal problems or your specific snafu. These services usually cost just a few dollars, if anything.

Finally, the best kept secret for the renter facing "the system" without a lawyer. In fact, I could lose my license for telling you this. (Okay, maybe not, but it sounds so darn dramatic.) The clerk's office. Those guys and gals behind the counter where they keep all the files, forms, records, twinkies, and chips are the secret. These people do not, and are not allowed to by law, give legal advice, but nobody knows the forms, special paperwork, and typical renter dispute better.

Don't be afraid to ask questions of the clerks. What paper do I need to file to sue my landlord to get my deposit back? What do I file if my landlord is trying to kick me out? Remember, the court clerk is not a lawyer and is not giving legal advice. But their non-advice can steer you in the right direction and sometimes the mechanics you need to get into and around the system are as important as knowing the law.

- Ask local law schools about free legal advisor service.

- Check with state and local bar associations for referral services and free law seminars.

- Work with court clerks to find out how to request the court's help and which forms to use.

LEGAL HELP FOR HOMEOWNERS

Unfortunately, owning a home often means bigger problems than those of the renter. Your financial investment is huge by comparison. Dealing with builders, real estate agents, and title companies is complex and the consequences of any mistake can be costly. This does not mean you can't follow some or all of the suggestions I've given for those who rent. In fact, neighbor disputes or fights with repairmen can feel and smell very much like the problems a renter has to handle.

The actual buying or selling of your home is a different story. If you sign papers promising to pay a person or a bank tens or hundreds of thousands of dollars, it's dumb not to spend a few hundred bucks keeping your assets out of trouble. So, hire a lawyer to go over all paperwork *before* you sign to buy your home. Hire a lawyer to go over all paperwork *before* you sign to sell your home. For $200 or $300, the attorney's seal of approval will be the cheapest insurance you can buy to protect your home purchase or sale.

This is never truer than when folks buy and sell homes with the help of title companies. These are the paperpushers and gatherers who check to make sure ownership of the property is in the right name, so some long lost relative of the former owner doesn't show up at dinnertime claiming he owns one of the bedrooms, part of the back yard, parking privileges in your driveway and 20 percent of your pot roast. You pay the title company to "clear" the title of these kinds of surprises. Title companies keep busy doing very important things and although they are working for you, they are not acting as your lawyer. When "closing time" comes around (that's the day all ownership papers are signed and legal ownership changes hands from the seller to the buyer), you'll feel much better if all title work and ownership papers have been reviewed by a professional working only for you. The title company has two clients, the buyer and the seller, and your interests are no more important to the title company than the other guy's. It's like a lawyer representing both the husband and wife in a divorce where it's more than likely somebody is going to get screwed. I'm sure the title companies will appreciate the comparison.

- Get professional help to review the home sale paperwork before "closing."

- Don't assume the title company is looking out for you.

- Don't forget to use law school advisors, referral services, and the clerk's office for less critical homeowner problems.

BEFORE FILIN' 'N' FIGHTIN'

You've tried being reasonable. Talking the problem over. Negotiating. You've even offered to work with an arbitrator or mediator to make things right. Unfortunately, the other guy hasn't read this book and he's a jerk. Now it's time to go to court.

Whether you get an attorney or go it alone, you have much work to do before filing your "complaint" (official word for lawsuit). You need to gather evidence, figure out who knows enough to be helpful as a witness, and get estimates or expert opinions about your damages. This is info you will use both to give the other guy one last chance to play nice and to present your case once you get to court.

I'll assume you are taking on the opposition without the help of a lawyer. Let's face it. If you have a problem big enough to justify hiring the big "L," you will be guided through this process, at a price per hour that is ten times the price of this book. Do what she says. She's the expert. If reading this book raises questions, ask your attorney, but don't second guess her actions, even if the information in these pages is the best, most down-to-earth explanation of how to survive and navigate the legal system you've ever seen.

Before filing your complaint, you will send a demand letter to the other side. This letter will be very polite, very straightforward and will chronicle the important events of your dispute.

Dear Rotten Neighbor:

I'm very sorry you've decided to act like the piece of human garbage you are. If you don't pay me for the damage your kids did to my yard, I'll be forced to take you to court. Instead, maybe I should just pour sugar into the gas tank of your car. I haven't decided yet which would be more fun. If I don't get the money by the end of the week, you'll find out.

Mr. Doe

Sending this letter will make you feel very good—for about a minute. That feeling will evaporate when you hear your letter read in open court at your small claims hearing. The judge won't like you. You'll look like an unreasonable, angry neighbor who probably deserved whatever he got. Being right will no longer matter. So, be nice.

Dear Mr. Smith:

On September 12, your children came onto my property and, with their bicycles, destroyed the plants and flowers in my front yard. Enclosed are pictures of the damage. Also enclosed is an estimate of the costs for replacement plants and labor charges required to return the yard to the condition it was in before your children damaged the property. This yard work must be done within the next two weeks to avoid further damage which might be caused by the expected winter weather. Consider this letter a formal demand for payment in the amount of $288. If I do not receive payment by October 10, I will file an action in small claims court.

Mr. Jones

Now this letter may not be as therapeutic as the first example, but it will be much more effective in court. This letter will become "Exhibit A" in your case. It tells the judge you did your homework, you acted professionally and gave the defendant/neighbor every opportunity to take responsibility without jumping at the first opportunity to involve the court. You will be liked by the judge and that's never a bad thing. If you still need to work out your aggression, take some of the money you get from your court victory and see a shrink.

- Track down the documents, pictures, and other evidence you'll need to prove your case.

- Do your homework and learn any special rules that apply to your case. This book is a good start.

- Send a focused, professional demand letter (not an irate letter) that includes a deadline for filing your complaint.

- Don't threaten to file a complaint if you don't intend to actually file.

THE COURT CLERK—YOUR NEW BEST FRIEND

You walk into the clerk's office. This is where you need to get the right form and pay your filing fee to start the process known as "litigation." There are tons of people standing in line. Nobody is happy about it. One of the first signs you see reads, "Do Not Ask the Clerks for Legal Advice." Your stomach does another 360 degrees. A lesser person would bolt for the door, but not you. You know that the info you need from the clerk isn't technically legal advice.

Approach the desk and just talk to the clerk about your case. Ask for a small claims complaint form. Ask about the details needed to explain your case in the right place on the form. Ask about getting the paperwork "served" (defined in the next section), which legally forces the other side to show up in court or lose the case. Ask if it's possible to file without paying a fee. Most places will let you file for free if you fill out another form explaining why paying would be a hardship. (You're only saving $10 to $20 bucks though, so you make the call.) You also get to add these and any other court costs to your claim against the defendant.

At some point, you will begin to annoy the clerk. Before you leave, or are assisted from the counter, make sure you pick a court date. I say "pick" a date because the clerk will usually let you do just that, if you ask nicely. Give yourself plenty of time to get the papers served on the defendant. Never sign up for a hearing date less than one month from the date you file. Oh, I know, you want to get in there and mix it up, but you'll need more time than you think to make sure papers are served properly and to pull together your presentation. Morning and afternoon court sessions are usually available.

- Don't be afraid to ask the court clerk questions.

- Ask about a waiver of the filing fee.

- Choose a court date (at least one month away) that is convenient for you.

GETTING A LEGAL GRIP ON THE DEFENDANT

Here's a nightmare. You're in court and the judge or bailiff calls your case. You are the only one to approach the bench and stand so very officially behind the counsel table. (By the way, the plaintiff always takes the table nearest the jury box. You won't get that in law school, or by watching *Law & Order.*) You feel pretty good. The defendant didn't even have the guts to show up. Then it happens. "Mr. Bryant, the file doesn't include proof the defendant was served. How was he served?" asks the judge. You gulp. "I'll take that as an 'I don't know'. Maybe you can come back when you figure that out," his Honor concludes. You slink out of court dazed and confused. There are several ways to avoid this rookie mistake.

"Service," no matter what the case or courtroom, means legally giving the defendant notice of your lawsuit. There are usually three ways to do that. The cheapest method is to send the paperwork certified mail, return receipt requested. The court clerk will often provide this service and charge you for it as part of the filing fee. Here's the problem with doing it on the cheap. Have you ever refused or ignored the mailman's attempts to deliver registered mail? If a person knows someone is out to sue, all that person has to do is say "no thanks," and the mail goes back to the court clerk. No Service.

If registered mail is the "horse and buggy" method of service, this next option is more like a dependable used car. You can have a friend or other person, not involved in the case, personally serve the defendant. This always raises the question, "I just have to touch him with the papers, right? Right?" Not exactly. Basically, you need to identify the person and leave the papers with him or her. You can drop them at the person's feet if you want. Let the weasel try to tell the judge how he wasn't "touched" with the papers. The judge will laugh, and if the defendant took the time to show up in court to make this argument, the judge is likely to hear the case, anyway.

Finally, you have the chauffeur-driven limousine approach to service. Call in the cops. More specifically, the sheriff. Most clerk's offices have a civil sheriff or constable who gets paid to deliver nasty court papers. You will pay about $20 to $30, but there is some satisfaction in knowing the service will get done right and it may shake up the other guy who gets a visit from the court cops while at work or hanging out at home. You can also pay a professional process server to do the same thing, but they don't wear uniforms or carry guns. What fun would that be?

From each type of service you will get a receipt as proof to show the court that the defendant got the paperwork. The beauty of this proof becomes very clear on the day of your hearing. If the defendant fails to show, you win. If he does show up and whines that he wasn't served properly, he's already in court and the judge is less likely to allow a re-scheduling. The judge wants to get it over with.

- The defendant must be "served" before you can argue your case.

- Use registered mail if you think the defendant will not avoid service.

- Pay a sheriff, constable, or private process server if you think the defendant will avoid service.

You've got the snappy suit, the fancy briefcase, and you've practiced using all the big words. Well, you won't need any of that stuff for small claims court. Tell Della to relax and put Paul on another case. You can handle this yourself.

Because home renter and homeowner problems are likely to lead you to small claims court, let's focus on that process. Personally, I love small claims court. It's so informal and so friendly compared to "real" court. The rules of evidence are usually relaxed or ignored altogether. Need to get a document or witness testimony in front of the judge? Give it a try. You're freed from the pesky rules that control and limit evidence in traditional court. Just how loose the judge plays with the evidence rules is up to that judge, the worst thing she might say is, "no." The judge knows you're not an attorney. She likes that. Be respectful and present your case as quickly and clearly as you can. Just tell the judge your story.

To do that, you need focus. Perhaps that means using an outline. Maybe you need to write out the whole story to be read in court. You can always use visuals to help your case. Pictures mounted on simple $8\frac{1}{2} \times 11$ inch paper with captions can be very effective. Remember, the judge has no clue what is going on, and you have only a few minutes to give her the facts and convince her you are right. Don't waste your time with details that don't mean anything.

The judge will probably ask you a few questions. Answer them briefly and directly. Use the time to sneak in a few tidbits you didn't get to in your opening explanation. Never argue with the judge. Persuasion doesn't mean raising your voice—to the judge or to your opponent.

Your evidence can include original lease papers, repair bills, or other paperwork. But bring along copies and give them to the court instead of the original documents. Witnesses are dangerous in small claims court, unless they have some info that you can't get anywhere else. You don't need a neighbor or relative to

KNOWING THE NUTS AND BOLTS

stand there and say, "Yep, Your Honor, it's just like she said." Think carefully about your need for witnesses.

Time to practice your spiel. Stand in front of a mirror or gather a few friends to listen. Pretend you are standing in court telling your story. The more comfortable you are in front of others, the better your presentation will sound when you get to talk to the judge in court.

Finally, invest a little time and go watch small claims court cases being tried before your hearing day. If you can't, go early on the date of your hearing and see how things work. It ain't no Judge Judy, or People's Court. More often than not, the judge won't even decide your fate on the day of the hearing. Some judges are just plain chicken. They don't want to look anybody in the eye and say, "You lose." So, the court takes the matter "under submission," and within a few days sends out the ruling by mail. It's like opening a report card. And you better know what to do with your passing or failing grade.

- Make an outline or write out your story to help you present your case to the judge.

- Use pictures or other visuals to explain the case.

- Avoid witnesses if possible.

- Take copies of the original documents to give the court and the other side.

- Practice your presentation in front of the mirror or in front of friends.

- Watch other cases being heard before you put on yours.

YOU'VE WON/YOU'VE LOST . . . NOW WHAT?

And the winner is? Hopefully, you. But, win or lose, don't panic. Nothing happens immediately. If you win, as a plaintiff, your first thought is, "How do I collect?" If you lose, as a plaintiff, your first thought is, "That judge isn't smart enough to understand my case. I want a new judge." A winning defendant just wants to forget the whole mess and a losing defendant also wants that "second chance." Can you appeal? Can you collect? You need to know your options.

As a losing plaintiff or defendant you have only one big decision. Do you want to appeal? An appeal is really just a request to tell your story to another judge, to be more convincing in presenting your position. But an appeal from small claims court is special. It may seem unfair, but often only the defendant can file an appeal from small claims court. It's one of those rules designed to streamline the system. Ask the court clerk if you, as a plaintiff, have the right to appeal. If plaintiffs are allowed to appeal, the rules are the same as for defendants.

As a losing defendant, the appeal means a new audience for your arguments. Often the appeal is really a new trial and the work you did in small claims court means nothing. You're starting over and you'll need to get the dog and pony ready for another show. In some courts the appeal is more formal than small claims court. You may be required to get an attorney. Talk to your new friend, the court clerk, about appellate details, like the important filing deadline. Figure you have 20 to 30 days, from notice of the small claims decision, to file your appeal.

Before filing any appeal, you should try one more thing. Talk to the other side. The thought of having to deal with the case again is not a happy one for anybody. Even the winner may be willing to compromise if it means staying out of court for the appeal. If the landlord won $200 in small claims court, offer him $100 right now to end the fight. Make sure you keep your promise to pay as quickly as possible, and get the winner to file the correct paper proving to the court that you have satisfied the judgment. (The form is usually called a Satisfaction of Judgment—see the clerk.)

Now, let's look at winning and collecting. You, the plaintiff, have won—and you want your money. Well, just take your notice of victory or "judgment" down to the courthouse where the judge in your case will personally pay you, in cash! Then take your money over to the Fantasyland Bank and make a deposit into your checking account. Oh, you detect a little sarcasm?

Nearly 75 percent of all small claims judgments go uncollected. That's three out of every four—uncollected. Here are basics on collecting. Your judgment is just a piece of paper that gives you, not the judge, not the sheriff, not your friend the clerk, the power to use the court to help you collect. There are three standard tools. You can go after the person's wages using "garnishment." You can try to seize or "levy" on bank accounts. You can put a "lien" on real estate by filing your judgment in any county where the defendant has property. The clerk's office will have the forms you need to use for any or all of these collection tactics. Ask for the right form and use your judgment paperwork from the court to fill in the information needed.

The sheriff's office or constable is your next step. These officers enforce your collection levy, garnishment, or lien by delivering the paperwork to the losing party's bank, employer, or person holding ownership rights to the property you want. You have to provide all the information, like bank account numbers or the address of the defendant's boss. The sheriff is not your personal Columbo. Oh, you'll pay a few dollars for the sheriff's services, too, but you can ask the court to add the amount to your judgment as "collection costs," without going back for another hearing. Ask the clerk for, yep, another form to get that done. Realize it is up to you to collect and your judgment is simply the court's blessing to knock yourself out doing it.

If you lost:

- Do you have the right to appeal?
- How much time do you have to file the appeal?

- Try to negotiate a settlement using your right to appeal.

- Be prepared for an attack on your assets if you don't appeal and you can't reach a compromise.

If you won:

- How long before you can start collection efforts?

- Go after bank accounts, wages, or property for collection.

- Become familiar with the sheriff's procedure for enforcing collection efforts.

PART

III

LANDLORDS AND TENANTS

Dear Michel:

My landlord is a real jerk. Will you please send me the renters and landlords rules or laws?

S.L.

Oil and water. Cats and dogs. Landlords and tenants. They just don't mix without a mess. You seldom hear, "My landlord is great!" "He's the nicest guy I've ever known." "I want to have my landlord's baby!" There seems to be natural friction when it comes to the relationship between one person collecting rent and the other person writing the check.

Most of the problems are caused by one thing: bad communication. Oh, sure there are landlords who have worked hard to earn their "jerk" reputation. Likewise, there are lots of tenants playing spoiled rock star and trashing the property of others. But, let's forget about them and focus on the communication in most situations. You look for a place, you find a place, you check out the place, you rent or lease the place, you decide to move from the place, the landlord keeps your deposit, and you start hollering.

3

FINDING A HOME TO RENT OR LEASE

ADVERTISEMENTS

Dear Legal Edge:

I read a newspaper ad about a quiet two-bedroom apartment near where I work. I moved in and haven't slept through the night since. What good are ads if they lie?

K.T.

L A W   A landlord's written representation in an advertisement is only an opinion, it is not a legally binding promise.

L I F E   We know that many advertisements are chock full of bull. Many homeowners-turned-landlords are getting more savvy about the ways of marketing. We see more private party ads filled with sales jargon such as, "New Condition," "Freshly Painted," "Re-Decorated." None of this means a thing. Here's a typical ad taken from a newspaper:

> *NICE, quiet, clean, large 3 bedroom, stove, fridge, new paint, laundry. Must See! $795*

Okay, so what does this ad tell you about the home? It tells you the owner or landlord is very pleased with the property and thinks you will be too. But the landlord's belief in the quality of the home is only an opinion. An opinion has no legal effect and gives you no protection. If you rush into renting this place, sign the lease, then learn the neighbors are in training for Jerry Springer audience-of-the-year, you won't be able to use the words in the ad as evidence of a legal promise. Take the ad with you to make sure any statement is more than just an opinion of the landlord.

And if you specifically ask the landlord about the neighborhood, the traffic, the noise, and you are told all is quiet, you have better protection. The difference? You have the right to rely on the eyeball-to-eyeball discussions you have with the landlord. The law recognizes and enforces specific representations you rely on before you sign a rental contract. Even better if you can get the landlord to put all representations in writing in the agreement itself.

How about the price in the ad? It's in your price range, but wouldn't it be nice to pay a little less? The ad price is just a solicitation by the owner or landlord. He wants you to pay that amount to rent the home. True, most people simply assume the rent is the amount advertised and sign the lease. Don't do that. This is a basic supply and demand situation. If the landlord needs your body in his home more than you need his home, you have a negotiating advantage.

Example: I was one of three guys trying to rent the same two-bedroom home. We were all looking around the place at the same time and the owner smelled blood. A regular bidding war was in the offing. I told the owner I would pay two months rent up front, in cash, and sign a one-year lease if he would drop the rent 5 percent. I also said the offer was only good until 5:00 p.m. that day, about three more hours. The other two guys couldn't top the offer without checking with significant others first. I got the home and for less rent than advertised.

- Take any advertisement or other written information about the home with you when you meet the landlord.

- Before signing any lease or rental agreement, ask specific questions about anything mentioned in the advertisement.

- Write down any representations made by the landlord.

- Don't be afraid to negotiate for a monthly rent that is lower than the advertised amount.

WORKING WITH A RENTAL AGENT

Dear Michel:

We thought that working with a rental agent would make getting a home easier. But we would hear one story from the agent and then learn the owner had changed his mind. We didn't know who to believe. We finally dumped the agent. Who do we believe?

D.H.

L A W   An agent speaks for the property owner. You have the right to rely on the things an agent tells you. You have the right to negotiate with and enter into any agreement with an agent, just as you would the property owner.

L I F E   We're talking here about rental agents who earn a commission showing potential tenants all kinds of different homes, not the folks who work as on-site property managers paid directly by the property owner. Rental agents cause problems. You're forced to deal with someone who has no interest in the property. Well, except for the commission that you pay as part of the artificially inflated rent. Remember one thing: the rental agent works for the property owner or landlord. The agent does not work for you, no matter how syrupy sweet the agent may be.

More important, working through a rental agent creates a greater possibility for confusion. "Yeah Mr. Owner, I told your agent-dude that we were going to dump our stuff on the 3rd and he said that was okay and we could blow off paying for the first two days of the month. Now you say we can't do that." Get any agent's promise in writing, dude.

- Make sure the agent has the power to negotiate for the owner or landlord.

- Make sure the agent puts any promises in writing before you sign the lease or rental agreement.

SURVIVING THE PROPERTY MANAGEMENT COMPANY

Dear Legal Edge:

We had some trouble with the property management company that we rented from. These companies really abuse their power. Our property manager would not remove a fridge that didn't work when we moved in three years ago. Then they threatened to evict us if we didn't remove it in three days. People need to know how to find out what to do if their management company is not playing fair.

S.E.

L A W   The property management company is governed by the same rules that apply to the landlord or property owner. The property management company simply steps into those shoes.

L I F E   A property management company handles tons of houses, apartments, and condos. They make money by getting a small percentage of the rent for each property. You tend to get lost in the shuffle. The actual person managing your home may change. The company may make new or different rules during the time you live in one of their properties. You may ask a question of Harry, only to follow up and find out that Mary is now handling the home you like. You're back to square one.

This is annoying when you're looking for a place, but becomes a huge problem after you've moved in. You need to be able to cut through the property management babble and get to the owner of the property. So, before signing any lease or rental agreement:

- Find out who actually owns the property.

- Check county records if the management company won't tell you.

- Send a copy of all letters, lease documents, or other similar materials to the property owner, even if you are dealing with the property management company.

4

APPLICATION—ACCEPTANCE— DISCRIMINATION—REJECTION

The process you have to go through to rent or lease a home these days is getting crazy. But you have to realize that there are just enough nuts and losers out there to make landlords skittish. And the property owner has the right to make sure you are not a socially-challenged tenant. If you think you've been treated badly, you then have the legal burden of proving that the rejection was discriminatory.

One more note about the application. Tell the truth. Say you fill out your application by stating that you are the supervisor at your job. So what if you're really the assistant to the assistant of the number one assistant? A harmless exaggeration by the tenant, right? Check the bottom of the application. (See the Rental and Credit Application sample form on pages 52–53.) You are usually signing an application promising the information is the truth. An exaggeration might give the landlord a legal argument to kick you out for lying. Don't do that. You're not running for president, there's no need to lie about your qualifications.

THE APPLICATION

Dear Legal Edge Guy:

I've just been told I can't rent the apartment I wanted. I filled out the application, paid for a credit check and now I think they're messing with me. What can I do and how can I prove discrimination?

H.H.

L A W   A landlord can legally refuse to rent to anyone for any reason, unless the decision is based on sex, age, race, religion, ethnic background, disability, or family status (renting only to those without children).

L I F E   Proving discrimination is your burden. It's not easy. Especially at the application stage. If all you have to go on is your "feeling" that you've been treated unfairly, you'll lose. Think about everything that happened during the entire application process.

Following are some indications that discrimination may be taking place. If you believe you have proof of discrimination, contact the U.S. Department of Housing and Urban Development.

- Did the landlord deny that an apartment or home was available, even though one was advertised for rent?

- Did the landlord say anything to suggest he wanted a certain race, sex, or other specific type of tenant?

- Were you told that you needed to make more money than seemed appropriate for the rent being charged?

The HUD folks will take your complaint, investigate, and put the screws to the landlord or property owner if they find evidence of discrimination. Will this help you get that apartment? Probably not. But, do you really want to live in a place where the landlord is a bigot or weasel? I don't think so. Keep looking.

RENTAL & CREDIT APPLICATION

PERSONAL INFORMATION

Name of Applicant: _____ Date: _____

Driver's License No: _____ SSN: _____

Current Address: _____

City: _____ State: _____ Zip: _____

How Long At Current Address? _____ Phone: _____

Name Of Current Landlord: _____ Phone: _____

Prior Address: _____

City: _____ State: _____ Zip: _____

How Long At Prior Address? _____ Phone: _____

Name Of Prior Landlord: _____ Phone: _____

How Many Adults In Family? _____ How Many Children? _____

Current Employer: _____

Job Title: _____ How Long At This Job? _____

Job Address: _____ Job Phone: _____

SPOUSE OR ROOMMATE INFORMATION

Name: _____ Phone: _____

Current Address: _____

Employer: _____ Job Title: _____

How Long At This Job? _____ Job Phone: _____

FINANCIAL INFORMATION

Name Of Bank: _____ Phone: _____

Address: _____

Checking Account No: _____ Savings Account No: _____

REFERENCES (Name, Address, Phone)

1. _____

2. _____

3. _____

RENTAL & CREDIT APPLICATION - Page Two

ADDITIONAL INFORMATION

Have You Ever Been Served Eviction Papers Or Been Asked To Move? _____

Have You Ever Filed For Bankruptcy? _____   If So, When? _____

Have You Ever Refused To Pay Rent? _____   If So, Why? _____

How Many Vehicles? (Including RV's, Motorcycles, Autos) _____

Please Provide: Make/Model, Year And License Plate Number For Each Vehicle

1. _____

2. _____

3. _____

How Did You Hear About This Home? _____

Address Or Unit You Wish To Rent Or Lease: _____

Do You Want To Lease Or Rent? _____ How Long? _____

When Do You Want To Move In? _____

DISCLOSURE AND CREDIT CHECK AUTHORIZATION

I/we, the undersigned, have been informed that _____ is the leasing or rental agent for the property owner or landlord and that any lease or rental agent fee will be paid by the property owner or landlord.

RADON GAS WARNING: Notice to prospective tenant- Radon is a naturally occurring radioactive gas that, when accumulated in a building in sufficient quantities, may present health risks to person who are exposed to it over a period of time. Levels of radon that exceed federal or state guidelines have been found in buildings in this state. Additional information regarding radon and radon testing may be obtained from your county public health agency.

I/We declare the information provided is true and correct, and I/We authorize you to conduct an employment and credit check and to verify our references.

Applicant: _____   Date: _____

Co-Applicant: _____   Date: _____

THE DREADED CREDIT CHECK

Dear Legal Edge:

My credit stinks. I know it will cause me problems when I try to rent my next apartment. How can I deal with this?

S.Y.

L A W   The landlord has no automatic right to check your credit. You must give your permission.

L I F E   Landlords and property owners want to know about your credit. The lease or rental application may include a credit check section, or it may be on a separate piece of paper. (See the Rental and Credit Application sample form on pages 52–53.) Do you have an ugly credit history? The decision to allow a credit check is yours.

The problem is this. If you don't allow a credit check, you don't get the apartment. The landlord has the right to make an informed decision about the person he takes on as a tenant. If his exercising that right gives you the willies, talk to the landlord about whatever it is that is bothering you. Many times they won't care that you had a bankruptcy four years ago, or that you made two late payments on your mom's electrolysis. In fact, they prefer the honesty. They will find out anyway, so why not turn a potential negative into a potential positive?

How about that credit check fee? Is it gone forever, even if you don't qualify for the home? Most lease agreements don't mention the fee or any rules that apply if your credit doesn't pass the landlord's test. Your potential new landlord will not refund your fee unless you get his promise to do so during the application stage. Ask how much the credit check costs, whether the landlord is keeping part of the fee and whether you get all or part of the fee back if the landlord doesn't like what he finds.

- Understand that you are giving the landlord the right to check your credit.

- Tell the landlord about any possible credit problems you expect to show up on the report.

- If you have to pay a fee for the credit check, try to negotiate a written promise that the fee will be refunded if you don't qualify.

YOU'VE BEEN REJECTED!

Dear Legal Edge:

Are there rules about the reason a landlord can give to reject you as a tenant? I know about discrimination, and I don't think that was it, but he didn't like something.

W.T.

L A W The landlord has a right to reject an applicant for any reason, so long as the decision is not based on illegal discrimination.

L I F E The most common reason for rejection is money. Not enough of it, too much owed to others, or trouble paying it back when you promised. You have the right to know why you were rejected. Ask.

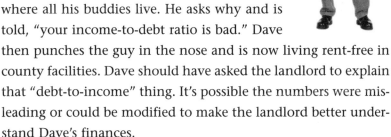

Dave is rejected at the apartment complex where all his buddies live. He asks why and is told, "your income-to-debt ratio is bad." Dave then punches the guy in the nose and is now living rent-free in county facilities. Dave should have asked the landlord to explain that "debt-to-income" thing. It's possible the numbers were misleading or could be modified to make the landlord better understand Dave's finances.

- If rejected, ask the landlord the reason, specifically spelled out in writing.

- Do not settle for a simple, "no," or "you don't qualify." Ask specific questions. Offer to supply further documentation or a higher down payment.

- Use your meeting with the landlord as a chance to sell yourself as a tenant.

5

THE LEASE OR RENTAL AGREEMENT

You've made it through the application process. Now the fun really begins. Are you leasing or renting? Is there a difference? Technically, yes, realistically, no. A lease is normally for a longer period of time. A six-month or one-year lease is what you'll encounter in most situations. "Renting" is the word normally given to places you live month to month. The only real difference is the period of time covered by the agreement or contract.

The following explains how each part of the lease or rental agreement works. Included is a typical agreement to follow. (See the Residential Lease Agreement sample form on pages 58–59). You will see the word "agreement" used instead of describing paperwork as either a "rental" or "lease" agreement, unless there is a special reason to do so. Don't sweat it. Remember the only real difference between leasing and renting is the length of time covered.

Reading and understanding the agreement is the single most important thing you will do when getting a new place. And you thought the most important thing was your sightline to the pool, shoe space in the closet, or the amount of sunlight

RESIDENTIAL LEASE AGREEMENT

THE PARTIES AGREE AS FOLLOWS:

_____ (Landlord) shall lease to _____ (Tenant) the property located at _____, in the City of _____, State of _____.

Term: This lease shall be for a period of _____ years, _____ months, beginning _____ and continuing through _____, unless terminated under the provisions of this Agreement.

Rent: Tenant agrees to pay landlord monthly rent in the amount of _____, to be paid on or before the first day of each month. Payment is to be made at _____, City of _____, or at any other place Landlord may request.

Security Deposit: Tenant agrees to deposit with Landlord the sum of _____, receipt of which is hereby acknowledged, as security for the faithful performance by Tenant of the terms of this Agreement. The deposit is to be returned to Tenant once Tenant has performed all provisions as promised.

Use Of Property: The property will be used by Tenant exclusively as a private residence, and neither the home or any part of the property will be used by the Tenant for the purpose of carrying on any business, profession, or trade of any kind. Tenant will comply with all laws, ordinances, rules, and orders of appropriate governmental authorities affecting the cleanliness, occupancy, and preservation of the property, during the term of this Agreement.

Condition Of Property: Tenant agrees that he has inspected the property, including the surrounding grounds and all buildings and improvements, and they are, at the time of the signing of this Agreement, in good repair, and in a safe, clean, and tenantable condition.

Number Of Residents: Tenant agrees that the property will be occupied by no more than _____ persons, including _____ adults and _____ children under the age of _____ years, without written approval from Landlord. No guest may remain longer than seven (7) days without prior written approval.

Quiet Enjoyment: Landlord promises that Tenant, upon payment of rent and performing the promises in this Agreement, will peacefully and quietly have, hold and enjoy the property for the term of this Agreement.

Utilities: Tenant will be responsible for arranging for and paying for all utility services required on the property, except _____, which will be provided by Landlord.

Assignment/Subletting: Tenant will not assign, lease or sublet the property without prior written approval of Landlord, whose approval will not be unreasonably withheld.

Improvements: Tenant will not make any improvements or alterations to the property without prior written approval. All improvements will become the property of Landlord unless those improvements are fixtures easily removed without damage to the property.

Damage To Property: If the property is damaged, due to some cause other than the acts of Tenant or Tenant's agents, Landlord will promptly repair the property, unless property is damaged so severely Landlord decides not to repair or rebuild and the property is no longer habitable.

RESIDENTIAL LEASE AGREEMENT - Page Two

Dangerous Material: Tenant agrees not to keep or store any dangerous, flammable, explosives or other materials that might increase the risk of fire on the property.

Animals: Tenant will not keep domestic or other animals on the property without written approval of Landlord.

Landlord Inspection: Landlord has the right to inspect the property at any reasonable time during the term of this Agreement.

Maintenance: Tenant will, at his expense, keep the property in good and sanitary condition during the term of this Agreement. Tenant will keep the furnace clean, keep walkways clean, and make all repairs to plumbing, heating, appliances and electric and gas fixtures if repairs are needed as a result of Tenant's misuse, neglect or some cause other than normal wear and tear. Major maintenance and repair, not needed as a result of Tenant's misuse or negligence, will be the responsibility of Landlord. Tenant agrees there will be no painting done or signs placed on the property without written approval of Landlord.

Subordination: Tenant's interest in the property is secondary to any lien or encumbrance.

Holdover: If Tenant remains in possession of the property, with Landlord's approval, after the term of this Agreement, a new month-to-month tenancy will be created and will terminate on _____ days written notice by Landlord or Tenant.

Surrender Of Property: When the term of this Agreement ends, Tenant will surrender the property to Landlord in as good a condition as the property was in at the time the parties entered into this Agreement, except for reasonable use, wear and tear.

Default: If Tenant defaults in the payment of rent or some other promise identified in this Agreement, Landlord may terminate this Agreement, re-enter the property and remove all persons from the property. Landlord will give written notice of any default and Tenant will have _____ days to correct any default and remain on the property.

Abandonment: If Tenant abandons property, Landlord may re-enter the property without being liable to Tenant for damages and may re-let the property and collect rent for the period remaining in this Agreement. Landlord will have the right to hold Tenant responsible for any difference in the rent collected following abandonment and the rent which would have been collected under the terms of this Agreement. Landlord may consider any personal property left by Tenant as Landlord's property and may dispose of such personal property in any way Landlord deems proper.

Binding Effect: The promises and conditions contained in this Agreement will bind heirs, legal representatives, and assigns of the parties. All promises are to be considered as conditions of this Agreement.

Other Terms:

NOTE: If you have any questions about the interpretation or legality of this Agreement, you may wish to seek legal assistance.

Landlord:_____   Tenant:_____

Date: _____   Date:_____

in the back bedroom for your little experimental garden. Wrong. Here's your chance to know more about the agreement than the landlord. Remember, most of these documents are written by attorneys for property owners, not tenants. The agreements are landlord friendly and terrible for the tenant. And the landlord has no legal duty to make sure you understand the agreement.

Finally. No matter what form it takes, you've got to have a written agreement. Yes, an oral agreement is binding, but proving the terms or rules of the deal is virtually impossible. *Don't do that.* Put it in writing. So, let's take a look at the important parts or clauses of the written agreement. Things you need to know before signing. How these rules impact your life as a tenant will be covered again in greater detail later on.

AGREEMENT TERM

Dear Michel James Bryant:
I'm not sure how long I want to stay in the next place I rent. I'm afraid to sign a lease because I might have to move fast. Any help?
H.E.

L A W   The agreement can include any term or length of time you will be living at the home. A one-month agreement is just as legal as a one-hundred year agreement.

L I F E   Signing an agreement to live somewhere for a certain period of time can be scary. Who knows what might happen or what you'll be doing in six months? For that reason, lots of folks shy away from leases and never sign up for longer than a month-to-month agreement. That's okay. But a longer term is not all bad.

When you sign an agreement for six months, a year, or longer, you and the landlord are promising that certain things will stay the same for the whole time you are leasing. Most important is how much you pay each month. A lease keeps the landlord from jacking up the monthly payment when you can least afford it. You can plan and budget better too. If you must go month to month, remember you are renting and any part of the agreement can be changed each month.

- Make sure the term of the lease or rental agreement is the length of time you want.

- Make sure you read and understand the agreement.

- Make sure the monthly payment doesn't change during the length of the agreement.

SECURITY DEPOSITS

Dear Legal Edge:

I'm confused about the reason I am giving the landlord a security deposit. Is it for rent? How do I know, when I first rent, exactly what it is for?

E.O.

L A W   A security deposit is supposed to protect the landlord in case the tenant causes property damage, or fails to do what the tenant promised in the agreement. The amount of the deposit may be controlled by local law, however the general rule is a deposit equal to one or two month's rent.

L I F E   There is no bigger battle between landlords and tenants than the security deposit. It is such a problem that we will get into the subject in ugly detail elsewhere in the book. (See "Where Is My Deposit?" on page 109.) But for now, we are looking at the agreement itself. There is normally no rule about the amount of the deposit, so negotiate. Hard up for cash? Offer to pay one half the deposit when you move in and the other half with your next month's rent. How far you can push will depend on how badly they need you. If the complex is full or you're one of five folks checking out the same home, your negotiations won't go far. But don't be shy. You're giving the landlord money he hasn't yet earned.

Speaking of earning. Are you getting interest on your deposit? Many states have laws requiring that your deposit is banked until you move out. Check your local housing authority or tenants' association to find out. But even without the law in your favor, you can always negotiate interest on the deposit. Too much trouble? Ah, what the heck, it's only your money. Do you want the landlord to invest it for his own profit? He will.

- Make sure the agreement includes the security deposit amount you've agreed to.

- The purpose of the deposit must be described.

- Negotiate payments on the deposit if money is tight.

- You may be entitled to interest on the security deposit.

PAYING RENT LATE WILL COST HOW MUCH?

Dear Legal Edge:
I just re-read my lease and figured out my landlord is gouging us $50 a month if the rent is two days late. Can he do that?
F.H.

L A W   The landlord cannot charge you a late fee unless the fee is part of the written agreement.

L I F E   The late fee is almost always included in the written agreement. That doesn't mean you have to accept the way it is written. If the agreement reads that you're late after five days, talk the landlord into a ten-day period. Or compromise at seven days. How much is the late fee? The law limits the amount of the fee, but the rule is fairly fuzzy. The fee can't be a penalty, whatever that is. Most courts have found that a 1 to 5 percent late fee is reasonable without feeling like a penalty. If you pay $750 for rent, then you'd pay $20 if late. The judge would probably okay that fee. If you know you're going to be late, talk to the landlord first to see if you can get a break.

- Do not pay a late fee unless the charge is part of your written agreement.

- You have the right to negotiate both the late fee amount and the grace period before the late fee can be charged.

- If you know you're going to be late, talk to the landlord first to see if you can get a break.

PETS

Dear Legal Edge:
I don't have any pets and don't plan to. Can't I just ignore the pets part of any agreement?

F.C.

L A W   The landlord has the right to evict you if you keep a pet that is not approved in the written agreement.

L I F E   The pet claws . . . that is, clause. Always good for a fight with the landlord. How is the clause written? Some say "no way" to pets without written permission from the landlord. If that's what you've got, make sure you get the okay before moving Fido or Fluffy into your place. Other agreements are less specific and there may be no mention of pets at all. If you have this less restrictive version in your agreement you may be able to get away with adding a pet after you've moved in, but it is risky.

How much is the pet deposit? There are no rules limiting the amount the landlord can charge so be prepared to negotiate. The smaller the animal, the less likely the damage and the less pricey the deposit. Figure $100 to $200 for a small dog or cat.

- Your agreement may require the landlord to give written permission before you bring home a pet.

- With no pet clause, you may be able to argue you don't need permission.

- Either way, prepare to negotiate the amount of the pet cleaning deposit before signing.

GUESTS

Dear Legal Edge:
I need a little flexibility in my new apartment. I have guests a lot and sometimes they stay for awhile. Is there anything I can do to get the landlord to be more flexible in his visitor rules?

D.S.

L A W   The landlord has the right to limit the number of guests and how long they stay in your home.

L I F E   Bring home a pet, bring home a guest. There isn't much difference. Sure, the pet may be cleaner and quieter. But, legally, your agreement can control the number of guests and how long they stay. If you break these rules, the landlord can try to evict you.

So, get rid of these landlord friendly rules. Or, at least, make them reasonable. If the rule says, "no guests," suggest you be limited to one or two. If the agreement says, "no more than two days," suggest one week. Most landlords really don't give a rip about good guests. But if the agreement is never challenged, this clause will sneak up and bite you. Deal with it before signing the agreement. Don't get bit.

- Check the agreement for "Guest" rules.

- Suggest more favorable rules before signing.

- Get any changes, in writing, in the agreement.

CAN YOU DO THAT AT HOME?

Dear Michel:

I'm so excited! I just started my own business out of my home. I do medical transcribing for doctors. It's just me and my computer and it's great! Now I need to move and I'm not sure if my new landlord will let me do this. Do I have a problem?

R.L.

L A W   The landlord has the right to control what you can and can't do, even in your own home, under the terms of the agreement.

L I F E   You're thinking, "Are we in a police state?" "Did we lose World War II?" How can the landlord control what I do in my own home? It's simple. You are going to live in a home owned by someone else. If you rented your garage to someone, you wouldn't want them to continue doing those monkey experiments, would you?

Fortunately, there is a limit to landlord control. If an activity is legal and does not noticeably affect the neighborhood, the agreement should not keep you from doing that activity.

- Check the agreement for limitations on your activities.

- If in doubt, ask about any activity that you have planned.

THE LANDLORD'S RIGHT TO DROP IN

Dear Legal Edge Guy:

At my last apartment I had a landlord who liked to pop in whenever he felt like it. I think he was trying to catch my girlfriend wandering around the place. I don't want that to happen in my new place. How do I keep things more private?

F.F.

L A W   The landlord has the right to come into your home under the terms of the agreement.

L I F E   You're in a romantic situation. The landlord barges in and, well, spoils the mood. You've had emotional problems ever since because his image is burned into your brain. This happens all the time. Now—before you sign the agreement—is the time to deal with this problem. The agreement may not say how much notice you get before a landlord pop-in, but the law says you need reasonable notice. Usually 24 to 48 hours.

- Check the agreement for the landlord's right to enter your home.

- Include a required 24- or 48-hour notice.

SUBLETTING

Dear Legal Edge:

I just signed a six-month lease last week. Today I got this great job upstate. I never really looked at the lease until now. It says "no sub-letting." I've got to move but I can't afford paying rent at two places. Did I mess up when I signed this thing?

S.G.

L A W   The landlord has the right to limit whether you can sublet or pass your agreement rights on to someone else.

L I F E   The last thing you're thinking about when looking for a new home, is the possibility you will need to move again. Start thinking about that possibility before you sign up. Can you sublet? When you sublet, you act as landlord and find another tenant to take over the rest of your agreement. Your agreement rules might not allow that to happen. Or the landlord may want to approve anyone you get to take over. Understand how much control you are giving up or negotiate around the restriction.

- Always plan for the unexpected need to move before the end of your agreement.

- Before signing make sure the agreement includes your right to sublet to someone else.

- Expect the landlord to ask for the right to approve the new tenant.

MOVING OUT

Dear Mr. Bryant:

The last time I moved I waited three months for the lousy landlord to give me back part of my deposit. With my next place I want to know what to expect before I rent.

T.K.

L A W   The agreement should explain the state law to be followed by the landlord, including the time limit to return your deposit and explain any deduction for damages or repair.

L I F E   The security deposit refund is the most common landlord-tenant fight there is. Tenants do most of the complaining. "The landlord kept my deposit for no reason." "I left the place cleaner than it was when I moved in." "It's been more than a month, where's my refund?" A lot of these complaints can be avoided if you work on the agreement.

Depending on your state regulations, the landlord has a limited time to return your deposit. You can figure two to four weeks in most cases. (See "Where Is My Deposit?" on page 109.) That info needs to be in your agreement now, at the signing stage.

- Ask the local housing authority about the refund time limit for your state.

- Before signing make sure the agreement includes the specific time limit.

MORE ABOUT YOUR AGREEMENT

You can be in such a hurry to rent or lease a place. But, that rush to judge an apartment will not acquit you of major hassles while you live in that home or when you decide to move on. The agreement is an important legal document. Only the purchase of a home or an expensive car is more important. A not-so-fancy apartment lease is a $10,000 commitment.

You may run into rules or clauses in your agreement that aren't covered in the sample agreement. Don't panic. Take your time to figure out exactly what the clause is all about. Ask the landlord. At the very least, he will be impressed that you've read the agreement closely enough to ask questions. If the landlord can't answer your questions, do not sign the agreement. Take the agreement home. Talk to your friends or co-workers. Everyone has a bad-landlord story. Check with an attorney. A simple agreement review won't cost that much.

6

YOUR LIFE AS A TENANT

You are very excited! You've just signed the agreement for your new place. Time to gather the friends who couldn't avoid helping you move. Let's fill this place up with junk! Hold your Water Pik. You have work to do before you move even one roll of toilet paper.

If we are understanding of the rights of both landlords and tenants, we can all learn to get along. Even so, there are a number of things that just seem to happen: rent increases, roommate changes, things that break, neighbors who annoy, pests, and pets. If all goes well, you survive these challenges, move on, and do it all again. Whether it's your first rental experience or your last, the big problems will seem smaller if you have . . . The Legal Edge.

THE WALK-THROUGH INSPECTION

Dear Mr. Bryant:
I know how important it is to inspect a home before moving in. But I can't get the landlord to do it. I can't wait forever.

K.P.

L A W   The landlord is not required by law to do a walk-through inspection of the home and may decide not to unless you demand the inspection.

L I F E   The walk-through inspection is for the protection of both the landlord and tenant. But it is your money he's keeping to cover damage beyond reasonable wear and tear. So who has more incentive? You do.

"Reasonable wear and tear." "Reasonable wear and tear." No matter how many times you chant this mantra, it means nothing unless you document the condition of the place before you move in. Reasonable wear and tear then has a starting point. A point that will be compared to the condition of the home when you move out.

At the very least, you must walk through the home with the landlord and his clipboard. If you are not familiar with the move-in checklist, see the Inspection Checklist sample form on page 71. Each room is checked and the list is marked and noted whenever and wherever you find a crack, chip, smudge, tear, burn, hair clog, or disgusting food fragment. Both you and the landlord will sign the checklist and you will get a copy. That's just the beginning.

Get your camera. Videotape is best, but photographs will work too. Buy a cheap disposable camera if you have to. One picture can be worth a thousand dollars or more. If you use a video, be certain to activate the date and time-stamp feature. For stills, have your photographs processed by a developer that dates the film. Take pictures of all fixtures. The toilets, sinks, shower, or tub. Appliances too. Take pictures of any damage already in the home. Now we're talking evidence. Proof of the condition of the home before you moved in. Keep the photos or videotape in a safe place with the checklist from the walk-through.

INSPECTION CHECKLIST

Resident's Name _____ Apt. No. _____
Building Address _____ Move-In Date _____
Date 30 Day Notice Received _____ Rent Paid Through _____
Forwarding Address _____ Move-Out Date _____

REMARKS   **MOVE-IN**   **MOVE-OUT**   **REMARKS**

                     Yes   No   Yes   No

Kitchen

REMARKS	Yes	No		Yes	No	REMARKS
_____	___	___	Refrigerator empty, clean	___	___	_____
_____	___	___	Meat container clean, unbroken	___	___	_____
_____	___	___	Ice tray clean, unbroken	___	___	_____
_____	___	___	Range, drip pans clean/unbroken	___	___	_____
_____	___	___	Tray, grill, present & clean	___	___	_____
_____	___	___	Oven clean & undamaged	___	___	_____
_____	___	___	Cabinets, shelves, closets clean	___	___	_____
_____	___	___	All wood & metal work clean	___	___	_____
_____	___	___	Sink dry & clean	___	___	_____
_____	___	___	Floors clean	___	___	_____
_____	___	___	Walls clean	___	___	_____

Living/Dining Room

REMARKS	Yes	No		Yes	No	REMARKS
_____	___	___	Drapes clean & undamaged	___	___	_____
_____	___	___	Carpet clean & undamaged	___	___	_____
_____	___	___	Walls & doors clean & unbroken	___	___	_____

Bathrooms

REMARKS	Yes	No		Yes	No	REMARKS
_____	___	___	Floors clean	___	___	_____
_____	___	___	Bathtub, lavatory clean	___	___	_____
_____	___	___	Towel rack present and hung	___	___	_____
_____	___	___	Mirror clean & unbroken	___	___	_____
_____	___	___	Medicine cabinet clean	___	___	_____
_____	___	___	Shwr door/tracks clean/unbroken	___	___	_____
_____	___	___	Fans & lights clean & unbroken	___	___	_____

Bedrooms

REMARKS	Yes	No		Yes	No	REMARKS
_____	___	___	Drapes clean & undamaged	___	___	_____
_____	___	___	Carpet clean & undamaged	___	___	_____
_____	___	___	Walls & doors clean & unbroken	___	___	_____
_____	___	___	Closets clean, rods present	___	___	_____
_____	___	___	Vanity area & mirror clean	___	___	_____

General

REMARKS	Yes	No		Yes	No	REMARKS
_____	___	___	Locks/keys present or returned	___	___	_____
_____	___	___	Screens/windows present, clean	___	___	_____
_____	___	___	TV leads present/undamaged	___	___	_____
_____	___	___	Patio swept & clean	___	___	_____
_____	___	___	All light fixtures clean/unbroken	___	___	_____
_____	___	___	Pest control required	___	___	_____
_____	___	___	OTHER	___	___	_____

SUMMARY_____
_____
_____

I certify that the subject apartment/house has been inspected and is in the condition noted.

_____   _____   _____   _____
Tenant   Date   Tenant   Date

_____   _____   _____   _____
Landlord   Date   Landlord   Date

Go through the same dance even if the landlord is a no-show because you'll still need evidence of the condition of the home when you moved in. Complete the sample checklist from this book. Don't let the landlord's laziness keep you from protecting your rights. Now that you're ready to move, don't forget to buy enough pizza for the folks helping you schlep your heavy furniture.

- Demand a walk-through before you move in.

- Flush all toilets, run hot water, and operate all appliances.

- Take photos or video of the home including all fixtures, appliances, and any damage to the home.

- Fill out the checklist carefully and completely.

- File the checklist, visual evidence, and agreement in a safe place.

RAISING THE RENT

Dear Michel James Bryant:
We have lived at the same place for 18 months. Next month the rent is going to go up. Is there any legal time period to give notice of a rent increase? Also, is there any limit to the amount the landlord can raise the rent?

R.A.

L A W   Except for a very few cities in four states (California, New York, New Jersey, Maryland) and the District of Columbia, the landlord can raise the rent as much as he wants. But, the landlord can't raise rent in the middle of your lease no matter where you live.

L I F E   It's not death. It's not taxes. But it's just as inevitable. If you live someplace long enough, the rent is going to go up. Especially if you have a month-to-month arrangement rather than a longer term lease. After two months you get the word, the rent is going up $50. If you rent month to month there is not a thing you can do. (Unless you live in one of those cities with rent control.)

There are two ways to create your own rent control. One: Before you sign any agreement, get a written promise that the rent won't go up for six months or one year. No kidding, this works. Even if you have a month-to-month agreement, you can convince the landlord that you will only rent the home if you get that promise. You end up with the benefits of a lease without being hooked into a long term agreement. Try it. You have nothing to lose. Two: Take the plunge and sign a lease. The landlord cannot raise your rent because it is fixed by the amount in your lease agreement for the length of the lease. You have the protection and you'll see that signing a lease is not as scary as you might think.

- Ask the landlord for the rental history of your home.

- If your agreement is month to month, ask the landlord for a written promise to hold rent steady for a number of months.

- If your agreement is a lease, make sure rent is not being raised in violation of the contract.

CHANGING THE RULES

Dear Mr. Bryant:
I have a question. After a lease is signed and given to you, can a manager or landlord alter or change it? What protection do I have as a renter?

S.C.

L A W   Once a lease or rental agreement is signed by the landlord and tenant, neither can change the terms unless the other approves the change.

L I F E   Up until the agreement is signed by both the landlord and the tenant, you can make all kinds of changes. It may start to look a little messy with all of the corrections, added words, and crossed out rules. (The crayon doesn't help, even though legal.) But changes before the agreement is signed are okay. This is all part of the negotiation process. Make sure you and the landlord initial any handwritten changes. Be aware that if you are dealing with the property manager or an on-site manager, he or she may not be authorized to make these changes.

You will never sign a standard lease or rental form contract without some changes. What? You've done that in the past? Can you still feel the wedgie you got from the landlord? Remember, form agreements are landlord friendly. You always want to negotiate changes to make the form more evenly balanced and tenant friendly.

The landlord may try to slip changes past you, after the agreement is signed. Is he trying to raise the rent? Trying to make you get rid of a pet? Does he want to move your parking spot? I don't think so. Refuse to make any changes. Of course, you always have the right to agree to the change if you'd like, but very few landlords want to make official changes that are good for the tenant. So why agree to a change that benefits only the landlord?

- Make any changes to the agreement before it is signed.

- Refuse, in writing, to agree to any changes the landlord tries to effect after signing.

BRINGING HOME A NEW ROOMMATE

Dear Legal Edge:
I'm getting a new roommate. I figured I would just handle the rent and bills myself and collect half from my roommate. What do you think?

D.W.

L A W Only the person who signs the lease or utility service agreement is responsible for payment. An unsigned roommate has no legal responsibility to pay.

L I F E It happens between friends. It happens between college roommates. It should never happen. Two people sharing the same place. One leaves and a new roomie moves in saying, "Hey, you just keep everything in your name and I'll pay you back for half each month." Unless you want to risk paying for long distance phone calls made by your new roommate to his girlfriend in Russia, your answer better be "Nyet."

If you are the original roommate, your name is on the lease or rental agreement. Your name is on the utility bills. That means only you are on the hook for rent, and for the phone and electric bills. Add the new roommate to all agreements. Then the landlord or the utility can look to either of you for the total amount due. That puts the pressure on both roommates to keep things paid up. The same is true if you have three or four people living together.

Sometimes landlords and utilities don't want to add new names to existing agreements. Or the landlord is being stinky about approving your new roommate. Now you need to write up your own little contract. Have the new roomie agree, in writing, to be responsible for a fair share of the rent and utilities. This is not as good as adding the new roommate to the original agreements, but at least you have a binding legal contract between you and the roommate, just in case the new roomie flakes. Remember though, the landlord and utility will still look only to you for payment and it would be your responsibility to go after the roommate based on your contract with that person.

- Check your lease or rental agreement rules for changing roommates.

- Ask the utility company how to add a new name to any agreement.

- Have your new roommate sign all agreements for rent or utilities, or sign a contract with you to share expenses.

WHEN THE TENANT ACTS LIKE A LANDLORD

Dear Mr. Bryant:

I understand about finding someone to take over my lease, but what if the person doesn't pay the rent on time or damages the place?

G.N.

L A W   If you move before the end of your lease, you normally have the right to find a replacement but you remain ultimately responsible.

L I F E   You get a new job. You find a great deal on a place across town. You lose a roommate. All of these are pretty good reasons to move. Even if you still have time remaining on your lease.

You need to sublet. Under the rules of most lease agreements, you have the right to find someone to take over your lease without paying a rent increase. That's because you are still responsible for the rent. So, to cut possible losses, you find a new tenant to sublet your place. You may be tempted to get just anyone. But that's not a good idea. Often, the landlord has the right to approve your choice. And, if the person stiffs the landlord or trashes the place, you could be responsible for rent and damages. So choose wisely.

- Confirm in lease agreement your right to sublet.

- Ask landlord to allow sub-tenant to pay rent directly.

- Ask landlord for promise not to raise rent for sub-tenant.

THE LANDLORD WILL FIND A REPLACEMENT

Dear Legal Edge:

I would like to find somebody to cover the balance of my lease, but I've got to move. Can the landlord sue me for rent for those last three months?

J.O.

L A W   In most cases, the landlord must try to find a new tenant if you move before the end of your lease.

L I F E   You may feel as if your lease is a prison sentence. No probation. No parole. That's not really true. If you have to break your lease and leave early, the warden—that is, the landlord—is going to help you out. Let's say you have three months left on your lease. You are technically responsible for those three months. But the landlord now must use "reasonable efforts" to find a new tenant for you.

What are "reasonable efforts?" Something between trying not to rent the place and holding an open house. Newspaper ads or signs would be reasonable. As soon as the landlord's efforts pay off, your responsibility for those leftover months ends. The landlord cannot get double rent. You will have to pay a price for the landlord's work, though. The cost of the landlord's "reasonable efforts," like newspaper ads, can be charged to you and billed or deducted from anything left of your security deposit. Keep an eye on the property so you know when it is occupied and your responsibility ends. Another option is to see if the landlord will let you buy off the balance of your lease at a fraction of the total.

- Remind the landlord of his duty to show "reasonable effort" in finding a replacement tenant.

YOUR HOME AS AN OFFICE

Dear Legal Edge:

My friend told me that I could be kicked out of the apartment I rent just because I started a home business. I'm working with small animals and I don't think the neighbors will mind. Can the landlord really do that?

R.C.

L A W   Either the landlord and/or local zoning laws can prevent you from running a business out of your home.

L I F E   There is nothing like commuting from your bedroom,
down the hall, into your office, in your pajamas. More and more
of us are working out of our homes. If you own your home, local
zoning laws can keep you from your work if it disrupts the neighborhood. If your business handles a large inventory, increases traffic, or has employees, you may be zoned out of business whether
you own or rent.

If you rent, you are also controlled by your agreement with the
landlord. Unless absolutely forbidden, you can usually operate a
low-key business from your home. The less you disrupt the complex or neighborhood, the better. If you have an envelope stuff-
ing business, nobody will ever know. But, if people are lining up
to have you train their dogs, that's tough to hide.

- Check your lease or rental agreement for limitations on
  home-based businesses.

- Check local zoning laws by contacting city hall.

- Any home business must have very little impact on the
  complex or neighborhood.

THE PROBLEM WITH PETS

Dear Mr. Bryant:

I know you always say not to hide things from the landlord because
it's worse if you get caught. Well, I did. I didn't think my bird would
cause any problems. What can the landlord do?

G.V.

L A W   If your agreement allows pets, you will be responsible for any damage they cause. If your agreement prohibits pets,
you can be evicted for breaking the rules.

L I F E   You love your pet. You treat the little guy like one of the family. So does the law.

First situation: Your landlord knows you have a pet and it's allowed in your agreement. If the mutt makes a mess, chews up the drapes, or bites a neighbor you will be expected to pay for damages, just as if a child caused the problems. Also, there is normally an extra deposit required. For your pet, not your child.

Second situation: You try to bring a pet into your place after you sign an agreement that does not include animals. Maybe you're trying to save the cost of the higher deposit. Maybe your landlord just hates animals and won't allow them. Maybe you visited the pound with a neighbor and had a love-at-first-sight experience. In any case, you can be evicted if you bring a pet home without the landlord's okay. Better to know, before filling the cat box, whether you and Fluffy get to stay.

- Check your lease or rental agreement to see if pets are allowed.

- If not, ask the landlord if you can add a pet to the lease.

- Ask for the landlord's definition of pet. Birds or fish may not count.

- Expect to pay additional deposit for possible pet damage.

LONG TERM GUESTS

Dear Legal Edge:
I have a friend staying with me. He keeps saying he won't be here much longer, but I'm getting nervous. I can't just tell him to leave. I owe him.

K.E.

L A W   The landlord has the right to limit the number of guests and the length of any stay.

L I F E   Everybody has friends, relatives, or other guests who come for a visit. But at a certain point, the visitor starts to look a lot like a tenant. That's when the landlord wants to know what's up. How long is too long depends on the agreement and the landlord, but common sense suggests that when a few weeks turns into more than a month, you've got a roommate. This is important for two reasons. First, you are responsible for anything your visitor does. Second, you may be giving your landlord  grounds to evict you for violating your agreement. Cheer up. You may want to use this rule to short circuit a visit from the in-laws.

- Check your lease or rental agreement for limits on guests.

- Let your visitor know the limits.

- Add your visitor to your agreement or suggest he or she move on.

NEIGHBOR TROUBLE

Dear Mr. Bryant:

I have a problem with the people upstairs. They have some kind of mental illness and they agitate me and my wife. They bounce up and down the stairs and slam doors as hard as they can. What can I do to stop this utter nonsense?

R.S.

L A W   The landlord is not legally responsible for the acts of other tenants, but does have a duty to enforce rules agreed to by tenants.

L I F E   Noisy, obnoxious, inconsiderate neighbors have been around since long before Ed Norton and Ralphie boy. When the situation gets unbearable, you have a few options. First, you can move. This may seem like the wimpy way out, but do you really want to live where the landlord won't do anything about the neighbors? And you can use the continuing commotion as a reason to break your lease.

Second, you may convince the landlord to evict the rude offenders. You'll need to help by making notes of the noisy events. Better yet, tape record what you hear.

Finally, talking directly to your neighbors is always worth a shot. Unfortunately, noisy, inconsiderate neighbors are not very receptive to the suggestion they pipe down. Still, give it a try if you think it will help.

- Give the landlord written notice of any noisy neighbors.

- Keep notes of the dates, times, and type of commotion.

- Tape record the noise your neighbors make.

HOME IMPROVEMENTS—YOURS OR THE LANDLORD'S?

Dear Mr. Bryant:

Our apartment is very hot in the summer but I can't afford to pay additional electric bills for running an air conditioner. I want to put a ceiling fan up in my bedroom. I'm sweating like a pig. Is that a problem?

S.B.

L A W   If you install lights or other fixtures that cannot be removed without damage, they become the property of the landlord.

L I F E   Turning the place you rent or lease into a "home" means adding personal touches. Some agreements say "no" to everything. No painting, no wallpaper, no trapeze equipment.

But, you're going to want to make changes if you stay in one place long enough. Paint and wallpaper are really not a problem. How about ceiling fans? Bookshelves? Sleeping lofts?

Here's the general rule: If what you do becomes part of the property, it is legally "permanent" and stays in the home when you move. The best example is carpeting or tile. Now, here's how to get around this rule. The real issue is damage to the property. You can install and take out light fixtures, fans, and maybe even shelving if you do it correctly. You may have a few holes to patch when you leave, but you are not permanently damaging the property if you can more or less restore it to its original condition.

Be careful, though. If you do this behind the landlord's back, you're giving him an argument to kick you out for violating the lease. You also take responsibility for messing up wiring or causing other damage. How badly do you want that ceiling fan?

- Check your lease or rental agreement for the rules on making improvements to your home.

- Permanent changes—attachment to the property and removal that causes irreparable damage—become the property of the landlord.

THE LANDLORD MAKES CHANGES

Dear Mr. Bryant:

I have an apartment with a fireplace. I have lived here for three years and now the fireplace is so dirty I can't use it safely. The landlord says he won't clean it. How can I get the legal edge to make the landlord clean the chimney?

V.J.

L A W   If your landlord removes amenities, or features, you expected as part of your lease or rental agreement, you may be able to break your lease or get a rent reduction.

L I F E   There are lots of reasons we choose a certain place to live. The ads scream out, "Exercise Rooms!" "Fireplaces!" Whatever the bait, we take it to get some of the goodies promised. But what if those goodies go bye-bye? If you really chose a home because of these extras, you have an argument that the landlord is not living up to his promises. That gives you two options. If the feature is important enough, you can try to get out of your lease. You need to convince the landlord you only moved in because of the fireplace.

Or you can ask the landlord to lower your rent. Why should you be paying higher rent for a place without an exercise room? You could have moved into the joint down the road to get the same thing for $100 less each month. Now you have to pay to join a local gym. You should get the price difference back in the form of lower rent.

Those are the arguments, but remember, the landlord may tell you to take a hike. And if the amenity now missing is important enough, you should. At least, you shouldn't get nailed for breaking your lease.

- Check your agreement to see if special features are listed as part of the "premises."

- Notify the landlord, in writing, as soon as you know the amenity is not working or unavailable.

- Plan to move unless you get a rent reduction or the amenity becomes available again.

WHO IS RESPONSIBLE FOR DAMAGE?

Dear Legal Edge:
My landlord just sent me a bill for fixing the dishwasher. I've lived here two years and I didn't do anything to break the machine. It's not like I throw food in there. Is the repair my responsibility?

R.A.

L A W　　The landlord is responsible for repairs that are needed due to "normal wear and tear." The tenant is responsible for all other property damage caused by the tenant.

L I F E　　You can see the fight coming. Who decides what is and is not "normal wear and tear?" A couple of examples may help.

There is a huge tree growing just outside the hall bathroom. Every year its roots find the sewer line and clog the flow, leading to an aromatic experience you would like to avoid. Cleaning out the sewer line is part of the normal use of the property. You haven't done anything to increase the amount of damage.

What if Junior is using the hall bathroom to develop film and print photographs? The dark room chemicals make the paint and wallpaper peel. These chemicals are not "normal" and you would likely pay for damage. Take it out of Junior's allowance.

- Before any activity, get an idea of what repairs the landlord will perform as "normal wear and tear."

- Try your best to put a "normal wear and tear" spin on the repair when you notify the landlord.

WHO IS RESPONSIBLE FOR INJURY?

Dear Legal Edge:
A friend of mine (I thought she was my friend) tripped and fell while running down the hall of my apartment building. Now she says it's my fault and I need to pay her medical bills. I don't have anything to do with the hallways. I think she's a klutz anyway.

C.B.

L A W　　The landlord is responsible for injuries caused by his negligence or wrongdoing over areas he controls.

L I F E　　You have a guest for a visit. On the way down to the pool, your visitor trips over a sprinkler hidden by an overgrown shrub. She cuts her leg and needs stitches. The landlord, two days earlier, told you he really needed to trim those bushes. Looks like a landlord problem.

Your guest gets back from the E.R. She climbs the stairs to your apartment and slips on the entry tile you just mopped. She does an encore at the emergency room. You might try to blame the landlord, but the wet tile and unprotected area was the real cause of the fall. That's your problem.

The focus on these examples is control. The landlord controlled the overgrown shrubs, you controlled the slick situation in your apartment. Of course, your guest is always responsible for his or her own injuries if caused by lack of care for his or her own safety.

- You or your landlord control the setting or surroundings where injury can occur.

- Maintenance or other records help show control over the area.

- Injured persons contribute to their own injury by acting carelessly.

THE LANDLORD BARGES IN

Dear Legal Edge:

My landlord feels he can come into our apartment anytime without asking. He walked into a neighbor's apartment the other day and scared a young lady. I found things from my closet all over my bedroom. The landlord said he has the right to come into an apartment if he thinks there is a potential problem. Something is not right.

A.G.

L A W   The landlord has no automatic right to enter your home. Notice is normally required unless you give permission or there is an emergency.

L I F E   There is something creepy about a landlord coming into your home whenever he wants. You could be in the middle of an important discussion, private moment, or lab experiment. You don't have to put up with that. The landlord gives up his right to enter your home at the point you sign an agreement.

But in that agreement, the landlord usually reserves the right to enter your home after giving you reasonable notice, normally 24 or 48 hours (also see pages 65–66). Emergencies are the other exception to the no barge-in rule. Fire, flood, something that requires immediate attention. Of course, you can always give the landlord permission.

No notice, no emergency, no permission—no entry by the landlord.

- Check your lease or rental agreement for the landlord entry rules.

- Notify the landlord immediately, in writing, if there is an entry without notice or permission, and remind the landlord of your privacy right.

- Remember that even landlord entry with notice can rise to the level of harassment if it happens too many times.

7

WHAT TO DO IF YOUR HOME ISN'T ALL IT'S SUPPOSED TO BE

Nothing is more frustrating than dealing with a broken home. Not the relationship-type broken home, but a home that is physically broken. You need to know how to have repairs done quickly, how to get your landlord's attention to make your home livable, or get her to reduce the rent.

DOING THE REPAIR AND DEDUCT

Dear Michel James Bryant:

I am living in an apartment complex and have a few problems. My living-room window won't open so I need to run my air conditioner a lot and my electric bill has doubled. Another problem. My garbage disposal backed up and I couldn't clean the sink for a week. I called the health department, but they wouldn't do anything. What can I do? Should I pay to have these things fixed?

M.L.

LAW The landlord is responsible for maintaining your home in a livable condition. If he fails to do that, you may be able to pay for the repairs yourself and deduct the cost from your rent.

L I F E   The kinds of problems you can take care of by repairing and deducting change from area to area and landlord to landlord. In some locales, only major defects can be repaired, like appliances, heating, cooling, or building leaks. But a jammed window that won't open could be a safety hazard. A broken window that won't close is a security problem. Maybe you can live without a garbage disposal, but should you have to?

The point? You can try the repair-and-deduct remedy on any problem if you do it right. That means giving the landlord written notice of the repairs you need. Forget the eighteen phone calls you made. Forget the five times you yelled at the landlord in the laundry room or parking lot. Put it in writing.

In your notice you will also give the landlord a time limit to fix the problem. The more serious the repair, the less time you give. If it's the middle of winter and the heater doesn't work, give the landlord 24 hours. If the refrigerator light went out, making it tough to tell how old that guacamole dip is, give the landlord two weeks. (Toss the dip in the meantime.)

Your notice will also tell the landlord your plan if he doesn't fix the problem. You have the right to hire a professional to do the repair. *Do not do the repair yourself.* Repeat after me: *I will not do the repair myself!* You risk making a bigger mess, you can't really put a value on your time like a pro can, and hiring an expert gives your repair claim credibility. Let the expert do the job.

There are some limits to the repair-and-deduct remedy. Don't rush out to spend your money on replacing a water heater or garbage disposal until you know those limits. Some states allow repairs totaling one month's rent. Some cities may put a dollar limit on repairs. These limits are usually high enough that they won't stop you from making typical repairs which are fairly cheap, less than $100.

The repair-and-deduct remedy is the most effective and powerful tenant tool to get the landlord's attention. Your written notice tells the landlord you're serious, you're smart, and you know your rights. At the very least, your written notice opens up communication that will lead to some resolution of the problem.

- Check with local housing authority for any limits to your right to repair and deduct.

- Give the landlord written notice of the problem, setting a time limit to make repairs and advising of your plan to repair and deduct.

- Hire a professional, pay for the repair and send the landlord a copy of the receipt with your reduced rent payment. Do not repair it yourself.

REDUCING YOUR RENT WITHOUT MAKING REPAIRS

Dear Mr. Bryant:

I've heard you talk on TV about making repairs and deducting the repair cost from the rent, but I don't have the money for the repairs. I'm lucky to make the rent each month. Any other suggestions?

R.P.

L A W   The tenant has the right to reduce rent if the landlord fails to repair problems violating local laws or building codes.

L I F E   It's true, using the repair-and-deduct remedy can mean money, temporarily, out of your pocket. You may be able to reduce your rent instead. The question is whether your home is habitable. Are there major problems that violate local or state building standards, such as roof leaks, electrical problems, or plumbing trouble? These repairs can be expensive. So, instead of paying for the repairs, you reduce your rent to the value of the home "as-is."

But, how do you figure out the value of your home with the broken shower? Good question. All you can do is estimate. Take a look at other rentals. Let's say you pay $550 for an apartment with two bathrooms. A one-bath rents for $475. A reasonable rent reduction would be $75.

Written notice is critical. Include a list of the problems and explain your plan to reduce the rent a certain amount each month until the repairs are completed. One warning: Do not use this remedy as a money saving scam when you don't have the money for rent. You're sure to get evicted when you're found out.

- Check with the housing authority for local or state building code standards.

- Estimate the value of your home "as-is" and calculate the reduced rent payment.

- Give the landlord written notice of problems explaining your plan to reduce your rent.

WITHHOLDING RENT

Dear Legal Edge:

When I moved into my apartment, it seemed clean, but now I have cockroaches. I talked to the landlord and he said that I must have brought the bugs with me. I don't have the money to move. What can I do?

D.H.

L A W   In a severe and desperate situation, a tenant may withhold the entire rent payment until the landlord provides the services and living conditions promised.

L I F E   Things are really bad. The roof leaks, the heat is out, the fireplace is clogged, and the only way to stay warm is to cuddle with your dog—and he has fleas. Or, you have bugs threatening the health and safety of your family. Desperate times call for desperate measures. Withholding rent will get your landlord's attention, but is that a good thing? The response may be an eviction notice.

To withhold rent, your home must be virtually unlivable. If it has some value as a shelter or place to sleep, it is better to pay that value, no matter how small. That having been said, don't be afraid to try and get the landlord to do what the law requires. Withholding rent hits the landlord right where he lives, the wallet. Just be aware that the attention you get might be an aggressive effort to get you kicked out of your home.

If you do withhold rent, it is a good idea to open a separate bank account to hold the dough. This move goes a long way toward showing the landlord you are acting in good faith and not just trying to avoid paying rent. You aren't just trying to get out of paying rent, are you? Make sure you mention this bank account when you give the landlord written notice of your plans.

- Give the landlord written notice of all problems and a time limit for repairs.

- Open a separate bank account for the rent you withhold.

CHAPTER

8

TIME TO MOVE

Your lease or rental agreement can come to an end in many ways. Sometimes it's your choice. Sometimes it's the landlord's choice. Sometimes it has little to do with either of you. No matter the reason, you need to know how to control what happens as your tenancy winds down. If you move at the natural end of your agreement, then getting your deposit back is all you care about. But if you are forced to leave before you're ready, or you want to leave against the landlord's wishes, then there is lots to talk about. Let's get to it.

WHEN YOU WANT OUT

Dear Legal Edge:

I'm not happy with my apartment and I'd like to break my lease. Do I have any choice but to stay for the remainder of my lease? I don't think I can find anyone to take over my lease.

T.N.

L A W   Assuming the landlord has provided all that was promised in your lease or rental agreement, you have an obligation to stay or pay through the end of your agreement, unless the home is occupied by a new tenant.

L I F E   It's not like taking a dress back to the store because it doesn't look right with your shoes. You cannot just move out of your place because you've changed your mind about where you want to live. Not without scrambling to come up with cash for the balance on your agreement or a new tenant to take over your lease. You're in better shape if you have a month-to-month agreement. All you need is 30 days notice and you're free. If you have to move more quickly than that, maybe losing a few days rent money isn't your biggest problem.

You've got more to think about if you have a typical six-month or one-year lease. Here are the options. First, if you honestly believe the landlord has treated you unfairly or has denied you the benefits promised in your lease, you can argue that you have a right to break the lease. You better have documentation to prove your case. Make notes and keep copies of any letters to the landlord or housing authorities supporting your claim.

Second, you can admit that you just need to move early and work with the landlord to get the place rented to a new tenant. That's important because your responsibility for the leftover months on your lease is cut off when you get a new tenant. Talk to your landlord. Find out how actively he plans to get a new tenant. Now is not the time to threaten the landlord into working harder on your behalf. Remember, he must use only "reasonable efforts" to replace you. Ask about newspaper ads, signs, or on-site promotion of your home. You will not help your cause by nagging the landlord.

Finally, you can try to sublet by finding a new tenant yourself. This is really a last resort unless you like the idea of playing landlord. You are stepping into the shoes of the landlord. Your name stays on the lease and you will still be on the hook for damages or unpaid rent. Not to mention the pain of trying to find your tenant. Don't do it if you don't have to. (Also see "When the Tenant Acts Like a Landlord," on page 76, which discusses subletting.)

One last note. Let's say all goes wrong. You have five months left on your lease and for whatever reason your old place stays empty. Now the landlord wants $2,500 for those five months. You can either wait for the landlord to sue you or you can try to negotiate a deal for less than the total unpaid rent. The landlord does not want to play *People's Court* with you and then try to collect. Offer her some cash to avoid court.

- Give the landlord written notice of the reasons, you believe, you have the right to break the lease.

- Work with the landlord to find a new tenant.

- Try to sublet the place yourself by stepping into the shoes of the landlord.

- Always monitor the old place to see when it re-rents.

- Negotiate a small buyout for the balance due on the lease.

NOW GET OUT!—YOU'RE BEING EVICTED

Dear Legal Edge:
Okay, I have been a little late with rent a few times. And then I got a dog but my lease doesn't say anything about pets, one way or the other. Now I get an eviction notice. I haven't been that bad. How bad is bad enough to get evicted?

D.C.

L A W   A tenant can be evicted for failing to do the things promised in the lease or rental agreement.

L I F E   It has such a nasty sound—eviction. Almost criminal. But you, as a tenant, can have legitimate reasons for breaking the promises you made in the agreement. Those reasons will become your defense to eviction if you decide to stay.

The mechanics of eviction. Every state has a very specific set of rules that must be followed by landlords to properly evict. It's nice to know there is a right and wrong way to kick somebody out onto the street. If you get an eviction notice, you better bone up on these rules. They vary from place to place, but the process is basically the same everywhere.

You normally get some warning that eviction is coming. It's called the "notice to pay or quit." (See the Notice to Pay Rent or Quit sample form on page 96) You either "pay" all back rent owed or you "quit" living in the home. Three days is the normal time period given to catch up on back rent. If you don't pay, the next notice you get will be the official eviction notice.

Once you get the eviction notice, better known as the complaint for unlawful detainer, the clock starts ticking on your time to respond. (See the Complaint—Unlawful Detainer sample form on pages 97–98.) The courts act quickly on these cases because they involve property possession. Judges want to get the landlord and tenant together fast to either give the property back to the landlord or allow the tenant to continue living in the home.

You normally have less than a week to file the correct response, or answer, to the eviction notice. (See the Answer—Unlawful Detainer sample form on pages 99–100.) Although a bit different in each state, the response you file will include the reasons you felt it was okay not to pay rent, or the reasons you refused to do whatever you didn't do under the terms of the agreement. The common causes for eviction are: stiffing the landlord on rent, damage to the property, major disruption of other tenants, having unofficial tenants, and bad pets.

NOTICE TO PAY RENT OR QUIT

TO: _____   DATE: _____

ADDRESS: _____

NOTICE: *To tenant and all others in possession of the premises described below. You*
are to quit, vacate, and deliver up the premises you hold as a tenant.

_____

_____

You are to deliver or vacate this premises within _____ days (excepting date of service, Saturday, Sunday, & legal holidays) of receipt of this notice, according to the appropriate state law of _____.

This notice is being given to you due to your failure to pay rent. You are currently behind in rent in the amount of _____ according to the following accounting:

You may reinstate your right to tenancy by full payment of this amount within _____ days (excepting date of service, Saturday, Sunday, & legal holidays). That date has been calculated as on or before the _____ day of _____, 19/20 _____, as provided under the terms of your lease or rental agreement or by the appropriate state law. If you fail or refuse to bring your rent payments current or vacate the premises, legal action will be taken immediately to evict you and to recover rents and damages for unlawful detainer of the premises together with any future rents due under the terms of your lease or rental agreement.

Landlord/Owner _____   Address_____

Agent _____   Phone_____

PROOF OF SERVICE
I, the undersigned, being at least eighteen years of age, declare under penalty of perjury that I served this notice to pay or quit tenancy, of which this is a true and correct copy, on the above-named tenant in the manner indicated below on _____, 19/20 _____:

_____ *I personally delivered a copy of the notice to the tenant.*
_____ *I mailed a true and correct copy of the notice to the tenant by certified mail.*
_____ *I mailed a true and correct copy of the notice to the tenant by first-class mail.*

Executed on _____, 19/20 _____, at _____

BY _____

ATTORNEY OR PARTY WITHOUT ATTORNEY (NAME AND ADDRESS):   TELEPHONE: | FOR COURT USE ONLY

ATTORNEY FOR (NAME):

insert name of court, judicial district or branch court, if any, and post office and street address:

PLAINTIFF:

DEFENDANT:

DOES 1 TO _____

| **COMPLAINT-Unlawful Detainer** | CASE NUMBER: |

1. This pleading including attachments and exhibits consists of the following number of pages: _____
2. a. Plaintiff is ☐ an individual over the age of 18 years.   ☐ a partnership.
      ☐ a public agency.   ☐ a corporation.
      ☐ other (specify):
   b. ☐ Plaintiff has complied with the fictitious business name laws and is doing business under the fictitious name
      of (specify):
3. Defendants named above are in possession of the premises located at (street address, city, and county):

4. Plaintiff's interest in the premises is ☐ as owner ☐ other (specify):

5. The true names and capacities of defendants sued as Does are unknown to plaintiff.
6. a.   On or about (date):   defendants (names):

      agreed to rent the premises for a ☐ month-to-month tenancy ☐ other tenancy (specify):
      at a rent of $ _____ payable ☐ monthly ☐ other (specify frequency):
      due on the ☐ first of the month ☐ other day (specify):
   b. This ☐ written ☐ oral agreement was made with
         ☐ plaintiff   ☐ plaintiff's predecessor in interest
         ☐ plaintiff's agent   ☐ other (specify):
   c. ☐   The defendants not named in item 6.a. are
         ☐ subtenants   ☐ assignees   ☐ other (specify):
   d. ☐   The agreement was later changed as follows (specify):

   e. ☐   A copy of the written agreement is attached and labeled Exhibit A.
7. Plaintiff has performed all conditions of the rental agreement.
8. ☐ a. The following notice was served on defendant (name):

      ☐ 3-day notice to pay rent or quit   ☐ 3-day notice to quit
      ☐ 3-day notice to perform covenant or quit   ☐ 30-day notice to quit
      ☐ other (specify):
   b. The period stated in the notice expired on (date):   and defendant failed
      to comply with the requirements of the notice by that date.
   c. All facts stated in the notice are true.
   d. ☐   The notice included an election of forfeiture.
   e. ☐   A copy of the notice is attached and labeled Exhibit B.
                     (Continued)

Form Approved by the
Judicial Council of California   **COMPLAINT-Unlawful Detainer**   CCP 425.12

COMPLAINT – Unlawful Detainer

Page two

9. ☐ a. The notice referred to in item 8 was served
   - ☐ by personally handing a copy to defendant on *(date)*:
   - ☐ by leaving a copy with *(name or description)*: ,a person
     of suitable age or discretion, on *(date)*: at defendant's ☐ residence
     - ☐ business AND mailing a copy to defendant at his place of residence on *(date)*:
       because defendant cannot be found at his residence or usual place of business.
   - ☐ by posting a copy on the premises on *(date)*: (☐ and giving a copy
     to a person residing at the premises) AND mailing a copy to defendant at the premises on
     (date):
     - ☐ because defendant's residence and usual place of business cannot be ascertained OR
     - ☐ because no person of suitable age or discretion can there be found.
   - ☐ *(not for 3-day notice. See Civil Code section 1946 before using)* by sending a copy by certified or
     registered mail addressed to defendant on *(date)*:
   b. ☐ Information about service of the notice on the other defendants is contained in attachment 9.

10. ☐ Plaintiff demands possession from each defendant because of expiration of a fixed term lease.
11. ☐ At the time the 3-day notice to pay rent or quit was served, the amount of rent due was $ _____
12. ☐ The fair rental value of the premises is $ _____ per day.
13. ☐ Plaintiff is entitled to immediate possession of the premises.
14. ☐ Defendants' continued possession is malicious, and plaintiff is entitled to treble damages. *(State specific facts supporting this claim in attachment 14.)*
15. ☐ A written agreement between the parties provides for attorney fees.
16. ☐ Defendant's tenancy is subject to the local rent control or eviction control ordinance of *(city or county, title of ordinance, and date of passage)*:

   Plaintiff has met all applicable requirements of the ordinances.
17. ☐ Other allegations are stated in attachment 17.
18. Plaintiff remits to the jurisdictional limit, if any, of the court.

19. PLAINTIFF REQUESTS
   a. possession of the premises.
   b. ☐ costs incurred in this proceeding.
   c. ☐ past due rent of $ _____
   d. ☐ damages at the rate of $ _____ per day.
   e. ☐ treble the amount of rent and damages found due.
   f. ☐ reasonable attorneys fees.
   g. ☐ forfeiture of the agreement.
   h. ☐ other *(specify)*:

_____   _____
(Type or print name)   (Signature of plaintiff or attorney)

VERIFICATION
(Use a different verification form if the verification is by an attorney or for a corporation or partnership.)
I am the plaintiff in this proceeding and have read this complaint. I declare under penalty of perjury under the laws of the State of California that this complaint is true and correct.

Date:

_____   _____
(Type or print name)   (Signature of plaintiff)

Page two

ATTORNEY OR PARTY WITHOUT ATTORNEY (NAME AND ADDRESS):	TELEPHONE:	FOR COURT USE ONLY
ATTORNEY FOR (NAME):		

Insert name of court, judicial district or branch court, if any, and post office and street address:

PLAINTIFF:

DEFENDANT:

ANSWER-Unlawful Detainer	CASE NUMBER:

1. This pleading including attachments and exhibits consists of the following number of pages: _____
2. Defendants *(name)*:

    answer the complaint as follows:
3. **Check ONLY ONE of the next two boxes:**
    - a. ☐ Defendant generally denies each statement of the complaint. *(Do not check this box if the complaint demands more than $1,000.)*
    - b. ☐ Defendant admits that all of the statements of the complaint are true EXCEPT:
        - (1) Defendant claims the following statements of the complaint are false *(use paragraph numbers from the complaint or explain)*:

            ☐ Contained on Attachment 3.b.(1).
        - (2) Defendant has no information or belief that the following statements of the complaint are true, so defendant denies them *(use paragraph numbers from the complaint or explain)*:

            ☐ Contained on Attachment 3.b.(2).
4. AFFIRMATIVE DEFENSES
    - a. ☐ *(nonpayment of rent only)* Plaintiff has breached the warranty to provide habitable premises. *(Briefly state the facts below in item 4.k.)*
    - b. ☐ Plaintiff waived, changed, or canceled the notice to quit. *(Briefly state the facts below in item 4.k.)*
    - c. ☐ Plaintiff served defendant with the notice to quit or filed the complaint to retaliate against defendant. *(Briefly state the facts below in item 4.k.)*
    - d. ☐ Plaintiff has failed to perform his obligations under the rental agreement. *(Briefly state the facts below in item 4.k.)*
    - e. ☐ By serving defendant with the notice to quit or filing the complaint, plaintiff is arbitrarily discriminating against the defendant in violation of the constitution or laws of the United States or California. *(Briefly state the facts below in item 4.k.)*
    - f. ☐ Plaintiff's demand for possession violates the local rent control or eviction control ordinance of *(city or county, title of ordinance, and date of passage)*:

        (Briefly state the facts showing violation of the ordinance in item 4.k.)

(Continued)

Form Approved by the
Judicial Council of California

ANSWER-Unlawful Detainer

CCP 425.12

ANSWER–Unlawful Detainer

g. ☐ Plaintiff accepted rent from defendant to cover a period of time after the date stated in paragraph 8.b. of the complaint.

h. ☐ *(nonpayment of rent only)* On *(date)*:   defendant offered the rent due but plaintiff would not accept it.

i. ☐ Defendant made needed repairs and properly deducted the cost from the rent, and plaintiff did not give proper credit.

j. ☐ Other affirmative defenses. *(Briefly state below in item 4.k.)*

k.   FACTS SUPPORTING AFFIRMATIVE DEFENSES CHECKED ABOVE *(Identify each item separately.)*

☐ Continued on Attachments 4.k.

5. OTHER STATEMENTS

  a. ☐ Defendant vacated the premises on *(date)*:

  b. ☐ Defendant claims a credit for deposits of $_____

  c. ☐ The fair rental value of the premises in item 12 of the complaint is excessive *(explain)*:

  d. ☐ Other *(specify)*:

6. DEFENDANT REQUESTS

  a. that plaintiff take nothing requested in the complaint.

  b. costs incurred in this proceeding.

  c. ☐ reasonable attorney fees.

  d. ☐ other *(specify)*:

_____   _____
(Type or print name)   (Signature of defendant or attorney)

_____   _____
(Type or print name)   (Signature of defendant or attorney)

*(Each defendant for whom this answer is filed must be named in item 2 **and** must sign this answer unless represented by an attorney.)*

VERIFICATION

(Use a different verification form if the verification is by an attorney or for a corporation or partnership.)

I am the defendant in this proceeding and have read this answer. I declare under penalty of perjury under the laws of the State of California that this answer is true and correct.

Date:

_____   _____
(Type or print name)   (Signature of defendant)

Page two

After you respond to the complaint, the court will set a date for hearing your arguments. You go in and tell your story. The landlord tells his. The judge makes a decision. If you lose, you move, and if you don't move, the court gives the landlord the power to throw you out physically, with the sheriff's help, if needed. If you win, you stay in your home, for now, but you can bet the defeated landlord will be even more fired up to get you out. So you might start looking for a new place anyway.

Win or lose, this whole process does one important thing; it buys you time. Even if you think you might lose the eviction battle, it takes at least a month to grind through the system. That time will help you figure out what to do. Find a new place, find a friend with a couch to surf, or get close with your family again. Use the time wisely.

- First eviction notice—to "pay or quit."

- Complaint for unlawful detainer—short time to respond to court.

- File your response, or "answer to complaint," and wait for court hearing date.

- Appear in court and argue against eviction.

- If you lose: Court may order sheriff to help landlord move you out.

- If you win: You can stay, but expect landlord to try again.

CONSTRUCTIVE EVICTION—IT'S A GOOD THING

Dear Legal Edge:
On Saturday, my neighbor set her apartment on fire. We had some bad smoke damage, but fortunately, nothing got burned. The fumes and smoke were horrid! We desperately need the place cleaned

and it has been long enough, especially since I have a ten-month old with asthma and she cannot tolerate being here. What can we do?

M.L.

L A W　When the condition of the property you rent or lease is virtually unlivable, the tenant has the right to move out without further responsibility for payments due under the agreement.

L I F E　Eviction is not always a landlord's weapon. A tenant can use "constructive" eviction to move out of a bad home without worrying about breaking the agreement. Cockroach stampedes, fires, soggy carpeting, and toilets that are only good for planters. Some tenants are too frightened to move under these conditions because they think they still owe money under their agreement. Landlords like that fear.

If living conditions are so bad that the health and safety of your family are threatened, move. In fact, you must move out to use a constructive eviction claim against the landlord. You can't stay in your home and still claim the home is unlivable. Make sense? But before you move, send the landlord written notice of the problems and your planned move out date.

- Give the landlord written notice of the problems that threaten the safety or health of your family.

- Then move out. You cannot stay in the home and claim constructive eviction.

- You must not have caused the unacceptable conditions.

CRIME AS A REASON TO MOVE

Dear Legal Edge:

I have six months left on my lease. In the time that I have been living here I have suffered about $4,500 in vandalism and the theft of my motorcycle and truck. Every couple of months someone comes through the parking lot slashing tires. Can I break my lease?

D.P.

L A W   A landlord is not normally responsible for the criminal acts of others, but the landlord's knowledge of criminal activity may be enough to allow the tenant to break a lease.

L I F E   The mere fact that you have been a crime victim is not the landlord's fault. But, let's say your car is vandalized or stolen and you later learn that the landlord knew of repeated rip offs but did nothing to keep it from happening again. Now you have an argument that the landlord should have done more to prevent the crime you suffered. Prove that argument and you may get out of the rest of your lease.

The reality is this. The landlord will not likely push you to the end of your lease if there is a crime problem at the complex. The case is a landlord-loser in court. What judge is going to force a tenant to remain in a crime-ridden environment?

- Learn all you can about the history of crime at the complex.

- Give the landlord written notice each time you suffer a crime.

- Give the landlord written notice that you are moving due to the crime problem.

WHEN THE HOME YOU RENT IS SOLD

Dear Legal Edge:

I woke up this morning to find a "For Sale" sign in the front yard of the home I rent. Shouldn't the landlord ask me about selling the house? I have months left on my lease.

H.U.

L A W   When property is sold, the rights and obligations of the landlord are normally passed on to the new owner of the home.

L I F E   It's a little scary to see a "For Sale" sign stabbed in the ground outside your rented or leased home. It's also annoying to deal with the lookey loo's checking out your place. Well, hang in there. The new owner must normally take over your lease or rental agreement and cannot evict you just because the property changes hands by sale. However, the new owner has no obligation to give you a new agreement when your current agreement ends. Kissing up to the new owner may help but has no legal effect.

- Check your lease or rental agreement for rules about sale of the home.

- Remind the current landlord of your interest in staying.

- Talk to the new owner about plans for the property when your current agreement ends.

WHEN THE BANK FORECLOSES

Dear Mr. Bryant:

I'm starting to wonder if my landlord is having money problems. The landscaping isn't being kept up and even minor repairs he used to do aren't getting done. Do I have any rights if the landlord is foreclosed on?

W.J.

L A W   The tenant's right to live in a home is cut off by a bank foreclosure, allowing the bank to evict the tenant.

L I F E   You may never know that the owner of the home you rent or lease is going belly up. The bank sends late notices to the owner, not to you. The sale is quietly done, normally without advertising. The first you hear about it may come in a letter from the bank telling you the property has been foreclosed on and, by the way, get out. This problem comes up in rented or leased houses, duplexes or condominiums, not traditional apartment buildings.

We're talking about something very different from the normal sale of property. Banks don't like being landlords. The bank has no obligation to continue your agreement because it is not controlled by your lease or rental agreement. That agreement normally includes the passage of your tenancy to a new owner if the property is sold. But, the bank is taking back the property, not buying it. Know the difference so you can avoid being surprised by foreclosure. If it does happen, you must be given reasonable notice to move. Normally, the same notice period required by your agreement.

- Be aware of hints of the landlord's financial trouble.

- The owner may foreclose on the home without notifying you.

- Check county records to see if property taxes are paid.

- Contact the foreclosing bank to find out if and when they plan to evict.

WHEN YOU JUST DON'T WANT TO LEAVE

Dear Legal Edge:
I just finished a six-month lease. I don't know how much longer I need to live here because I am getting a divorce. Is there any way I can stay for a while without a new lease?

F.S.

L A W   When a tenant stays beyond the end of a lease or rental agreement, the landlord can either evict or continue accepting monthly rent payments.

L I F E   It's called "holding over." For some reason you just don't want to leave even though your lease or rental agreement has ended. Maybe you're lazy, or you want the kids to finish school with their friends, or you're making the moves on a new neighbor.

What you need to know is that most of the rules are the landlord's to use. He can immediately start eviction proceedings if he wants. Most often, the landlord will continue to accept monthly payments until you decide whether or not to stay, unless your place is already promised to someone else.

Understand that a very important change in your rights as a tenant has occurred. No matter how many months or years were on the agreement that expired, you are now a month-to-month tenant. You may even pay more each month that you "hold over" because the landlord is no longer controlled by the terms of your expired agreement. Better move or get a new agreement signed right away.

- Tell the landlord as soon as you know you plan to "hold over."

- Check your agreement for the rules on staying beyond the end of that agreement.

- Either move or sign a new agreement as soon as possible.

THE MOVE-OUT INSPECTION

Dear Michel James Bryant:
We are getting ready to move from the apartment we rent, but we can't get the landlord to come over and walk through with us. Should we just leave without his inspection?

H.R.

L A W   The lease or rental agreement usually gives the landlord and tenant the right and responsibility to join in an end of tenancy inspection or walk-through.

L I F E   The move-out walk-through is just as important as the move-in inspection. Why is it that so many tenants blow them off? Sometimes it's because the landlord is tough to find or won't schedule the time. Sometimes you're in a big hurry, you've got a new place waiting, and the move itself is taking all your time. Don't ignore it. Do not leave your old place without doing an inspection. It is the best way to prove the only damage to the home is "normal" or "reasonable wear and tear." Remember, you pay for damage that goes beyond the norm. Doing the walk-through will give you the strongest argument to get your entire deposit back.

Let's cover the two possibilities. First, you meet with the landlord and do the inspection. Go to your file cabinet, desk drawer, or check behind the really old box of Cocoa Puffs to find the original walk-through checklist you filled out when you moved in. Use this as a guide. Go room to room pointing out to the landlord the items already listed as damaged before you moved in. Make sure you get a copy of the move-out checklist from the landlord. If you don't agree with the landlord's version of the inspection, immediately dispute any marks, chips, broken tile, glass, or other items the landlord claims you damaged. Do it in writing.

Now get the video or still camera. It's about time you finish off that roll of film you started last year, anyway. Take pictures of every room and any specific area that the landlord has marked on the checklist as damaged. Next, take fiber samples from the carpeting and get them to the lab for analysis. . . . Oh, sorry, got carried away.

The second possibility is that the landlord won't meet you for the move-out inspection. That's his problem. But you still need to fill out the checklist and take the pictures just as if the landlord had come along. You'll need all that evidence and more if you end up fighting over your deposit.

Basic rule: the landlord who is too busy to do a walk-through is the landlord who will rip you off by keeping most or all of your deposit.

- Move-out inspection helps guarantee return of your deposit.

- Schedule the move-out inspection with the landlord.

- Use your move-in checklist as a guide.

- Take photos of all rooms and specific damage.

- Do your own walk-through even if the landlord is a no show.

CHAPTER

9

AFTER THE MOVE

You've moved. You packed up the books, had the carpet shampooed, left the key in the mailbox. You didn't look back, you're gone. With any luck, you won't have to think about your former home again. Most tenants aren't so lucky. The number one complaint against landlords? Cheating a tenant out of all or part of the security deposit. If you've done your homework and use the following info, you can avoid being a victim.

WHERE IS MY DEPOSIT?

Dear Legal Guy:

In August we moved out of our apartment, leaving it in better shape than when we moved in. We called the landlord to see when we were getting the deposit back. The landlord told us we weren't getting our deposit back because there was a chip in the bathtub. We had never seen the chip and swear it was not there when we left. Now what?

B.B.

Dear Mr. Bryant:

We cleaned our butts off when we moved out of our apartment. But the landlord says he spent the whole deposit to clean up. What's the deal and how do we get this guy?

B.G.

Dear Legal Edge:

I cleaned up, moved out and turned in my keys more than a month ago. Doesn't the landlord have to send me my deposit, or do I have to go get it?

D.A.

L A W   The landlord must give you, within a reasonable time, a refund of your deposit less any itemized deductions for rent or damage beyond "normal wear and tear."

L I F E   The landlord has a tremendous advantage because he has your cash. That puts you in the position of coming after him and the money. Luckily, almost every state puts a specific time limit on how long your landlord has to return your deposit.

Deposit	*$500*
Carpet Tear	*– 75*
Stained Drapes	*– 60*
Repainting	*– 100*
Total to Tenant	*$265*

Deposit Refund Statement

Usually between two and four weeks. Along with your refund must be a list itemizing any deduction from the deposit. See example above.

If you disagree with the landlord's list or the amount of your refund, you need to make the next move. First, send the landlord written notice of your difference of opinion. Remember that checklist and the pictures you took? Send copies of each to the landlord with your letter. Make it nice. Your letter will become "Exhibit A" if you have to take the landlord to small claims court. You'll want the judge to know that you are calm, cool, and deserve to collect. Check local law for possibility of punitive damages against the landlord for wrongfully withholding deposit money.

- Ask the landlord how soon to expect your deposit refund.

- Check with the local housing authority for the exact time limit in your area.

- Send a written notice to the landlord describing any deposit deduction you contest.

- Send copies of photos and the checklist to prove condition of the home when you moved.

WHEN THE LANDLORD WANTS MORE

Dear Mr. Edge:

We just got a letter from the landlord. We thought it was our deposit refund but instead we got a list of damage charges and a bill for $301.00. How can the landlord do this when we know we didn't do the damage?

P.D.

L A W   If your deposit is too small to cover legitimate damages or unpaid rent, you can be sued by the landlord.

L I F E   The tenant has moved. The landlord goes to the home to find the garage door hanging by one hinge and the microwave oven missing. She throws her head back and laughs out loud. Something she learned in therapy. Then she sends the former tenant a bill for $975. It happens. You may owe the landlord more than the deposit you paid when you first moved in.

Unless you've decided to beat a hasty retreat out of town, you can fight over the bill your landlord sends. One of two things will happen. Either you will sue the landlord, just as you would for any dispute over the refund of a deposit. Or the landlord will sue you for the damages he claims you caused to the property. In response to the landlord lawsuit you make your own claim for your deposit refund.

- Review the damage claim exceeding your deposit made by the landlord.

- Try to work out a compromise before getting help from the court.

- Prepare to sue or be sued by the landlord.

MEETING THE LANDLORD IN SMALL CLAIMS COURT

Dear Legal Edge:

I've never been to court, but I need to go now to get my security deposit back from my landlord. I think I have the necessary papers and pictures. Any other suggestions?

Y.P.

L A W   Both the landlord and the tenant have the right to ask the court to decide any dispute over deposit refund or property damages.

L I F E   When all else fails, you go to small claims court. You've tried talking it over. You've sent your letter, photos, and checklist trying to convince the landlord you're right. Still nothing. Now it's time to ask the judge for help. The detail and mechanics of small claims court are covered in a separate section of this book. But there are a few special tips that can help you present your tenant case or defend against a landlord claim.

Preparation is everything. Collect your checklist from the move-in and move-out inspections. Make copies. (One woman took original uncashed checks to court as evidence. The court kept them for months.) Make copies of anything that helps your case.

Mount any photos on $8^1/_2$ x 11 paper or cards. Your goal is to make the judge's job easy. You won't get all day to whine and moan. So, make it short and sweet and hope the judge appreciates how professional and unemotional you are about your case.

Witnesses. Not a great idea. Ask yourself if the info your witness provides is really new and different from what you have to say. The witness's knowledge must be firsthand, not something your witness knows because you told him or her. The more impartial the witness, the better. Your best friend or sister may be great for moral support, but leave them in the courtroom audience.

You may have noticed there is no distinction drawn between preparation to fight for your deposit and preparation to fight against your landlord's claim. No need. The same documents, photographs, and testimony will be evidence that you left the home as you should have.

Prove that and you'll get back more of your deposit—or you'll beat back any claim by the landlord.

- Take to court copies of your move-in and move-out checklist.

- Mount any photographs on paper or cards, including descriptions.

- Be sure you need witnesses before taking any to court.

FIGHTING OUTSIDE THE COURT

Dear Legal Edge:

I'm having trouble getting my deposit back from my landlord, but

I've heard horror stories about small claims court. I don't want to waste my time. What else can I do?

E.L.

L A W   Both the landlord and the tenant may decide to have their dispute settled without going to court. The lease or rental agreement may even require an alternative.

L I F E   Somewhere between a friendly compromise and the court are the alternative dispute-resolution animals known as arbitration and mediation. You can use these alternatives to settle your fight. In fact, you may be required to. Check your lease to see if you've waived your right to go to court. Take a look at chapter 1 to learn more about arbitration and mediation.

- Check your agreement to see if you are required to use arbitration or mediation.

- Check your local housing authority for low-cost arbitration or mediation services.

- Prepare for arbitration or mediation just as you would for small claims court.

MY EX-LANDLORD SAYS WHAT?

Dear Mr. Bryant:
I think my last landlord hates me. It would take pages to go through all that happened, but my question is, what can he say about me when I try to rent again? Do I have the legal edge?

R.S.

L A W   The landlord must not falsely represent your payment history or the reason you moved from your former home.

L I F E   You may not give a rip what your old landlord thinks about you, but your new landlord wouldn't mind his opinion. If you were late a few times with your rent, don't let your new land-lord learn that from your ex-landlord. Be honest. Explain why you were late and convince the new landlord it won't happen again.

Face it. If you were evicted from your old place for good reason it will be tougher to get into the new place. You wouldn't want you as a tenant. Do your best to explain how things are different now and hope your new landlord is more understanding.

The real problem: When a landlord lies about the reason you left your last home. You may have a case against your old land-lord for defamation (a lawsuit based on injury to reputation), but that won't help you get into the new home you want. Be pre-pared to give the new landlord evidence of your sparkling his-tory as a tenant. Timely dated rent payment receipts or checks, walk-through inspection checklists, photos (yes, again with the photos)—the same stuff you might use in court, arbitration, or mediation, to prove you have been and are a good tenant.

- Be honest about any negative rental history the new landlord is bound to discover.

- Use documents and photos to dispute a bad reference and convince the new landlord that your tenant history is clean.

CONCLUSION

It's a long haul from the day you started looking for a home to rent or lease to the day you moved out and moved on. No mat-ter where you are in that journey, the law is there to help.

Prevent problems by reading, understanding, and customiz-ing your lease or rental agreement before your sign. Inspect the home using the checklist and photos to document the condition before you move in. Talk with the landlord about problems that pop up during the time you're a tenant, then cover yourself with a written follow-up. And take the time to protect your deposit by documenting the move-out condition with more photos.

If you give the landlord the benefit of every doubt, you'll be sorry. Much better to expect the worst, do what you need for protection, and then hope you never have to use your tenant's rights against the landlord.

IV

YOUR HOME:
BUYING, LIVING, SELLING

Dear Legal Edge:

We are finally ready to buy our first home. After renting for so long we really need to know what to expect. How do we get the legal edge?

F.O.

It is still the American dream: owning your own home. In many ways it's more challenging than renting. More responsibility. More risk. But there is something about owning that piece of dirt and the walls surrounding you and yours. The paint is peeling, but it's your paint. The roof needs a little work, but it's your roof. The backyard is full of dog poop, but it's your . . . hey you don't have a dog . . . it's your neighbor's animal. Still, even then, you are proud. It's your home, and since the days of the Midwest land grab and before, we have worked hard to own a small piece of the world in which we live.

There are three very important but very different phases of home ownership. You buy. You live there. And if you are like most, at some point, you will sell. Buying means lots of paperwork and important decisions that will affect your home purchase for years to come. Living in your home is like renting until something goes wrong and your level of responsibility increases dramatically. And selling is . . . well, selling a home is unlike any other experience in life. We'll get to that.

Through the questions and concerns of folks from across the country, we will explore all three areas to give you an idea how to handle the small problems and prevent those troubles from getting worse. Let's just say that owning a home is a learning experience. Like having and raising kids. You can read all the books. You can talk to experts. But until you go through the different steps, stages, and struggles of home ownership you will not truly appreciate the journey. Unlike parenting, your home ownership duties will not require late night feedings or diaper changes.

10

BUYING YOUR HOME

FINDING THE RIGHT HELP

Dear Mr. Bryant:

My sister just bought a home and didn't use a real estate agent. Is that smart? Wouldn't an agent be working for her and protecting her? Who's paying for that big car anyway?

D.K.

L A W   The real estate agent is normally under contract to the seller, not the buyer. The agent's primary legal responsibility, then, is to the seller.

L I F E   Have you ever seen a real estate agent driving around in a Yugo? It won't happen because in the real estate biz a big flashy car says, "I sell a hell of a lot of homes." We want to be around this sales greatness. Realtor-Home Buyer. It is the strangest relationship. You cruise around in the real estate agent's car. The agent chats with you and shows you homes for sale by all kinds of people. The agent seems to care about your needs, and maybe he or she does care. You would like to think so. But the agent is almost always being paid by the home seller and has a legal duty to act in the best interests of the seller, not you, the buyer. Did you sign a contract with the agent to help you buy a home? Nope.

That doesn't mean you should avoid using a real estate agent. In fact, they help you for free! Let the agent do the legwork tracking down the kind of home you want. Let the agent narrow down the homes in your price range. Just remember the agent only makes money when a home is sold. The more money the agent gets for the home seller, the bigger the commission. If you want to hire a real estate agent to represent you as a buyer, that can be done, for a fee.

- The real estate agent has a legal duty to the home seller, not the home buyer.

- Ask to see other homes the agent can show you, not only homes that she represents (which mean a bigger commission).

- Hire an agent to represent you if you are uncomfortable only dealing with a "seller's" agent.

KNOWING THE NEIGHBORHOOD

Dear Legal Edge:

When we went house hunting we thought we checked out the neighborhood. After moving in we learned that the Army Corps of Engineers is blasting down the street and will be for at least a year. We're really rattled.

C.I.

L A W The home seller or his agent is required to tell you about problems on the property you are buying. Investigating the neighborhood is normally the responsibility of the buyer.

L I F E While the discovery of neighborhood blasting may be a bit extreme, many home buyers learn too late about trouble on the block. Lots of crime, heavy traffic, the guy next door who always walks around outside wearing only his underwear. There are no specific rules forcing the seller or his real estate agent to check out the neighborhood, so you better make sure you know what you're getting into.

Visit the area at different times of the day—and night. Knock on a few doors. Question the police. Tell your potential neighbors you're thinking of moving into the area and would like their opinion of the neighbors and neighborhood. No matter what they report, you'll have the chance to size up the neighbors directly. If they're not your kind of people, for whatever the reason, you may decide not to buy the home next door. Sounds snooty? This is serious business. Do you want to invest your money and years of your life living in an area that makes you uncomfortable? Besides, you may want to live next door to the guy in the underwear. So take the time to get to know the neighborhood before you buy.

- Neither the realtor or the seller is required to tell you about the neighborhood.

- Check out the neighborhood at different times of the day and night.

- Ask local police about the crime rate.

SHOULD I BUY NEW OR OLD?

Dear Legal Edge:

We're so excited about buying our first house, but we're not sure we want to buy someone else's problems. That's what we think we might be doing if we don't buy new. What do you think?

E.K.

L A W   Because disclosure laws are virtually identical for new and existing homes, the only real difference is the new home warranty.

L I F E   The decision to buy or build a new home versus buying an existing home is 90 percent personal and 10 percent legal. Disclosure laws, which will be covered later, will help you get the information you need before you make your home purchase. For now you should know that the rules are basically the same for new and existing home sales. You will be told about known defects, flood potential, pests, and things like homeowner associations.

With a new home, you have greater warranty protection for two reasons. First, the home is a "product," so certain product warranty protections automatically apply. At the very least, you will have a one-year warranty on the home and specific warranties on the appliances, heating and cooling equipment, and fixtures that may run for more than one year. Some roofing materials are warrantied for fifty years or life.

Second, most builders these days provide an extended warranty of up to fifteen years. This is an insurance policy normally paid for by the builder as an incentive to get you to buy their product. The new trend is to offer extended warranties even for existing homes, but these policies are more restrictive in the claims they can make. If you are enticed by the promise of an "extended warranty," make sure you ask the builder or seller for the written warranty. The whole thing, not just a pamphlet. You need to know about the limitations and specific coverages. Let us know if you find one that covers doggie damage to bathroom plumbing. Don't ask.

- Disclosure laws apply to both new construction and existing homes.

- New homes are automatically covered by better warranties for products in the home and for the home itself.

- Ask about extended warranties.

- Find out who pays for the coverage and read about any limitations.

WE'RE BUILDING OUR DREAM HOME

Dear Legal Edge:

We've always wanted to have a new home built just for us. I have one friend who hated the whole experience and one friend who loved the construction process. What do I need to know?

G.J.

L A W   While building a new home your rights and responsibilities are controlled by a construction contract.

L I F E   New home construction: You either love it or hate it. Are you a detail person? Do you enjoy checking up on people? Do you have the extra beer you'll need to lubricate the subcontractors working on your new home?

Protecting your rights begins long before the start of construction. You will negotiate and sign a very expensive contract that covers everything from the total square footage of the home to the number of light switches in the third bedroom. The more detail in the contract the better. You will usually be given "allowances" for things like floor coverings, plumbing fixtures, and landscaping. These "allowances" are spending limits. If you are allowed $1,000 for carpeting but later find out it will cost $2,000 for the floor covering you want, you'll pay an extra $1,000 out of your pocket. Why is this important? The person lending you the money wants to know, before you start building, how much money you need and where it's going. Let's say your loan is for $100,000. The lender is not going to keep changing the loan amount every time you go over budget on one of these allowances. If you plan on using some special linoleum in the kitchen, get the price figured into the contract up front to avoid begging the banker to increase your loan or digging deeper into savings.

Get more than one bid or estimate for construction. Three is a good number. Each contractor should have the exact same material to review to make the bid. The same blueprints, the same materials list, the same information about location. Then start comparing. Is one using better wood? Is one contractor building a bigger patio area? The lowest bid means nothing, technically, if the contractors are building different homes.

Finally, you will ask your home builder all the same questions you ask of a home improvement contractor. In fact, new home construction is really the ultimate home improvement. (Also see "Congratulations! It's a New Bedroom," on page 180, which deals with licensing, permits, bonding, and insurance.)

- Get bids from three different contractors.

- Your construction contract will include very specific information about any "allowances" or spending limits.

- Check on licensing, permits, bonding, and insurance.

GETTING THE TRUTH, THE WHOLE TRUTH AND NOTHING BUT THE TRUTH

Dear Michel James Bryant:

This whole home buying thing is my wife's idea. I don't mind humoring her, but I'm afraid we might buy a well-disguised disaster. What exactly are we to expect to be told by the seller or realtor?

W.J.

L A W   The law requires that the seller or agent tell you about structural defects, potential problems like flooding, and any other fact that might negatively affect the value of the property.

L I F E   If you rely only on what the law requires others to tell you, you're in trouble. The "disclosure" laws are a good start. Is the roof bad? You must be told about it. Electrical or plumbing problems? You must be told about them. The home is built on "Love Canal Court" or "Three Mile Island Avenue?" Someone better talk. But these kinds of problems are obvious, and if you weren't told about them directly, you'd find them during your inspection.

If a realtor is involved, you will also receive an official disclosure statement. (See the Real Estate Transfer Disclosure Statement sample form on pages 126–127). Read it carefully. This form is very detailed and can be used as a great guideline no matter where you buy your home. As good as it is, it's not good enough.

Ask questions in writing and get answers in writing, from the realtor or the home seller. "How many times have you called a plumber in the time you've owned the home?" "What repairs were done?" "Have you ever made any repair to the home, due to fire, flood, or other event?" "Have you ever made a claim of any kind on your homeowner's insurance and what was the nature of each claim?" Not only are these questions direct, but the answers can be checked out through insurance or service records—something that may become very important if you buy the home and later have to take the seller to court for fraud. The message is clear: Don't jerk me around Mr. Seller. Or would you prefer to drop the price of the home another 30 percent?

- Ask the seller or agent if they are following federal and state disclosure rules.

- Read any disclosure statement carefully.

- Ask additional, specific questions in writing and get written responses from the seller.

TAKE A PRO WHEN YOU LOOK AROUND

Dear Legal Edge:

We watched your TV program about the things home buyers have to be told by sellers. We've done all that with the seller of the house

CALIFORNIA
ASSOCIATION
OF REALTORS®

REAL ESTATE TRANSFER DISCLOSURE STATEMENT
(CALIFORNIA CIVIL CODE 1102, ET SEQ.)

THIS DISCLOSURE STATEMENT CONCERNS THE REAL PROPERTY SITUATED IN THE CITY OF _____
_____, COUNTY OF _____, STATE OF CALIFORNIA,
DESCRIBED AS _____.
THIS STATEMENT IS A DISCLOSURE OF THE CONDITION OF THE ABOVE DESCRIBED PROPERTY IN COMPLIANCE
WITH SECTION 1102 OF THE CIVIL CODE AS OF _____, 19____. IT IS NOT A WARRANTY
OF ANY KIND BY THE SELLER(S) OR ANY AGENT(S) REPRESENTING ANY PRINCIPAL(S) IN THIS TRANSACTION,
AND IS NOT A SUBSTITUTE FOR ANY INSPECTIONS OR WARRANTIES THE PRINCIPAL(S) MAY WISH TO OBTAIN.

COORDINATION WITH OTHER DISCLOSURE FORMS

This Real Estate Transfer Disclosure Statement is made pursuant to Section 1102 of the Civil Code. Other statutes require disclosures, depending upon the details of the particular real estate transaction (for example: special study zone and purchase-money liens on residential property).

Substituted Disclosures: The following disclosures have or will be made in connection with this real estate transfer, and are intended to satisfy the disclosure obligations on this form, where the subject matter is the same:

☐ Inspection reports completed pursuant to the contract of sale or receipt for deposit.
☐ Additional inspection reports or disclosures: _____
_____

II
SELLER'S INFORMATION

The Seller discloses the following information with the knowledge that even though this is not a warranty, prospective Buyers may rely on this information in deciding whether and on what terms to purchase the subject property. Seller hereby authorizes any agent(s) representing any principal(s) in this transaction to provide a copy of this statement to any person or entity in connection with any actual or anticipated sale of the property.

THE FOLLOWING ARE REPRESENTATIONS MADE BY THE SELLER(S) AND ARE NOT THE REPRESENTATIONS OF THE AGENT(S), IF ANY. THIS INFORMATION IS A DISCLOSURE AND IS NOT INTENDED TO BE PART OF ANY CONTRACT BETWEEN THE BUYER AND SELLER.

Seller ☐ is ☐ is not occupying the property.

A. The subject property has the items checked below (read across):

☐ Range	☐ Oven	☐ Microwave
☐ Dishwasher	☐ Trash Compactor	☐ Garbage Disposal
☐ Washer/Dryer Hookups		☐ Rain Gutters
☐ Burglar Alarms	☐ Smoke Detector(s)	☐ Fire Alarm
☐ T.V. Antenna	☐ Satellite Dish	☐ Intercom
☐ Central Heating	☐ Central Air Conditioning	☐ Evaporator Cooler(s)
☐ Wall/Window Air Conditioning	☐ Sprinklers	☐ Public Sewer System
☐ Septic Tank	☐ Sump Pump	☐ Water Softener
☐ Patio/Decking	☐ Built-in Barbecue	☐ Gazebo
☐ Sauna		
☐ Hot Tub ☐ Locking Safety Cover*	☐ Pool ☐ Child Resistant Barrier*	☐ Spa ☐ Locking Safety Cover*
☐ Security Gate(s)	☐ Automatic Garage Door Opener(s)*	☐ Number Remote Controls _____
Garage: ☐ Attached	☐ Not Attached	☐ Carport
Pool/Spa Heater: ☐ Gas	☐ Solar	☐ Electric
Water Heater: ☐ Gas	☐ Water Heater Anchored, Braced, or Strapped*	
Water Supply: ☐ City	☐ Well	☐ Private Utility or
Gas Supply: ☐ Utility	☐ Bottled	Other _____
☐ Window Screens	☐ Window Security Bars ☐ Quick Release Mechanism on Bedroom Windows*	

Exhaust Fan(s) in _____ 220 Volt Wiring in _____ Fireplace(s) in _____
☐ Gas Starter _____ ☐ Roof(s): Type _____ Age: _____ (approx.)
☐ Other: _____

Are there, to the best of your (Seller's) knowledge, any of the above that are not in operating condition? ☐ Yes ☐ No. If yes, then describe. (Attach additional sheets if necessary.): _____

B. Are you (Seller) aware of any significant defects/malfunctions in any of the following? ☐ Yes ☐ No. If yes, check appropriate space(s) below.
☐ Interior Walls ☐ Ceilings ☐ Floors ☐ Exterior Walls ☐ Insulation ☐ Roof(s) ☐ Windows ☐ Doors ☐ Foundation ☐ Slab(s)
☐ Driveways ☐ Sidewalks ☐ Walls/Fences ☐ Electrical Systems ☐ Plumbing/Sewers/Septics ☐ Other Structural Components
(Describe: _____
_____)
If any of the above is checked, explain. (Attach additional sheets if necessary): _____
_____

*This garage door opener or child resistant pool barrier may not be in compliance with the safety standards relating to automatic reversing devices as set forth in Chapter 12.5 (commencing with Section 19890) of Part 3 of Division 13 of, or with the pool safety standards of Article 2.5 (commencing with Section 115920) of Chapter 5 of Part 10 of Division 104 of, the Health and Safety Code. The water heater may not be anchored, braced, or strapped in accordance with Section 19211 of the Health and Safety Code. Window security bars may not have quick release mechanisms in compliance with the 1995 Edition of the California Building Standards Code.

Buyer and Seller acknowledge receipt of copy of this page, which constitutes Page 1 of 2 Pages.
Buyer's Initials (____) (____)   Seller's Initials (____) (____)
The copyright laws of the United States (17 U.S. Code) forbid the unauthorized reproduction of this form by any means, including facsimile or computerized formats.
Copyright © 1990-1997, CALIFORNIA ASSOCIATION OF REALTORS®. In compliance with Civil Code Section 1102.6 Effective July 1, 1997.

Published and Distributed by:
REAL ESTATE BUSINESS SERVICES, INC.
a subsidiary of the CALIFORNIA ASSOCIATION OF REALTORS®
525 South Virgil Avenue, Los Angeles, California 90020

┌─ OFFICE USE ONLY ─┐
Reviewed by Broker
or Designee _____
Date _____

REAL ESTATE TRANSFER DISCLOSURE STATMENT (TDS-14 PAGE 1 OF 2) REVISED 3/97

Reprinted with permission, California Association of Realtors.® Endorsement not implied.

126

Subject Property Address: _____ Date _____

C. Are you (Seller) aware of any of the following:

1. Substances, materials, or products which may be an environmental hazard such as, but not limited to, asbestos, formaldehyde, radon gas, lead-based paint, fuel or chemical storage tanks, and contaminated soil or water on the subject property . . . . ☐ Yes ☐ No
2. Features of the property shared in common with adjoining landowners, such as walls, fences, and driveways, whose use or responsibility for maintenance may have an effect on the subject property . . . . ☐ Yes ☐ No
3. Any encroachments, easements or similar matters that may affect your interest in the subject property . . . . ☐ Yes ☐ No
4. Room additions, structural modifications, or other alterations or repairs made without necessary permits . . . . ☐ Yes ☐ No
5. Room additions, structural modifications, or other alterations or repairs not in compliance with building codes . . . . ☐ Yes ☐ No
6. Fill (compacted or otherwise) on the property or any portion thereof . . . . ☐ Yes ☐ No
7. Any settling from any cause, or slippage, sliding, or other soil problems . . . . ☐ Yes ☐ No
8. Flooding, drainage or grading problems . . . . ☐ Yes ☐ No
9. Major damage to the property or any of the structures from fire, earthquake, floods, or landslides . . . . ☐ Yes ☐ No
10. Any zoning violations, nonconforming uses, violations of "setback" requirements . . . . ☐ Yes ☐ No
11. Neighborhood noise problems or other nuisances . . . . ☐ Yes ☐ No
12. CC&R's or other deed restrictions or obligations . . . . ☐ Yes ☐ No
13. Homeowners' Association which has any authority over the subject property . . . . ☐ Yes ☐ No
14. Any "common area" (facilities such as pools, tennis courts, walkways, or other areas co-owned in undivided interest with others) . . . . ☐ Yes ☐ No
15. Any notices of abatement or citations against the property . . . . ☐ Yes ☐ No
16. Any lawsuits by or against the seller threatening to or affecting this real property, including any lawsuits alleging a defect or deficiency in this real property or "common areas" (facilities such as pools, tennis courts, walkways, or other areas, co-owned in undivided interest with others) . . . . ☐ Yes ☐ No

If the answer to any of these is yes, explain. (Attach additional sheets if necessary.) _____
_____
_____

Seller certifies that the information herein is true and correct to the best of the Seller's knowledge as of the date signed by the Seller.

Seller _____ Date _____

Seller _____ Date _____

III
AGENT'S INSPECTION DISCLOSURE

(To be completed only if the Seller is represented by an agent in this transaction.)
THE UNDERSIGNED, BASED ON THE ABOVE INQUIRY OF THE SELLER(S) AS TO THE CONDITION OF THE PROPERTY AND BASED ON A REASONABLY COMPETENT AND DILIGENT VISUAL INSPECTION OF THE ACCESSIBLE AREAS OF THE PROPERTY IN CONJUNCTION WITH THAT INQUIRY, STATES THE FOLLOWING:

☐ Agent notes no items for disclosure.
☐ Agent notes the following items: _____
_____
_____

Agent (Broker Representing Seller)_____ By _____ Date _____
                                   (Please Print)   (Associate Licensee or Broker Signature)

IV
AGENT'S INSPECTION DISCLOSURE

(To be completed only if the agent who has obtained the offer is other than the agent above.)
THE UNDERSIGNED, BASED ON A REASONABLY COMPETENT AND DILIGENT VISUAL INSPECTION OF THE ACCESSIBLE AREAS OF THE PROPERTY, STATES THE FOLLOWING:

☐ Agent notes no items for disclosure.
☐ Agent notes the following items: _____
_____
_____

Agent (Broker Obtaining the Offer)_____ By _____ Date _____
                                   (Please Print)   (Associate Licensee or Broker Signature)

V

BUYER(S) AND SELLER(S) MAY WISH TO OBTAIN PROFESSIONAL ADVICE AND/OR INSPECTIONS OF THE PROPERTY AND TO PROVIDE FOR APPROPRIATE PROVISIONS IN A CONTRACT BETWEEN BUYER AND SELLER(S) WITH RESPECT TO ANY ADVICE/INSPECTIONS/DEFECTS.

I/WE ACKNOWLEDGE RECEIPT OF A COPY OF THIS STATEMENT.

Seller _____ Date _____   Buyer _____ Date _____

Seller _____ Date _____   Buyer _____ Date _____

Agent (Broker Representing Seller)_____ By _____ Date _____
                                                        (Associate Licensee or Broker Signature)

Agent (Broker Obtaining the Offer) _____ By _____ Date _____
                                                        (Associate Licensee or Broker Signature)

SECTION 1102.3 OF THE CIVIL CODE PROVIDES A BUYER WITH THE RIGHT TO RESCIND A PURCHASE CONTRACT FOR AT LEAST THREE DAYS AFTER THE DELIVERY OF THIS DISCLOSURE IF DELIVERY OCCURS AFTER THE SIGNING OF AN OFFER TO PURCHASE. IF YOU WISH TO RESCIND THE CONTRACT, YOU MUST ACT WITHIN THE PRESCRIBED PERIOD.

A REAL ESTATE BROKER IS QUALIFIED TO ADVISE ON REAL ESTATE. IF YOU DESIRE LEGAL ADVICE, CONSULT YOUR ATTORNEY.

┌─ OFFICE USE ONLY ─┐
Reviewed by Broker
or Designee _____
Date _____

EQUAL HOUSING
OPPORTUNITY

Page 2 of 2 Pages.

REAL ESTATE TRANSFER DISCLOSURE STATMENT (TDS-14 PAGE 2 OF 2) REVISED 3/97 we're buying. Isn't that enough? Do we really need to pay for an inspection? And what kind of inspection are we talking about?

D.H.

L A W   An independent home inspection is the buyer's last chance to make sure he isn't buying a defective home and allows the buyer to get out of a contract if the home does not pass that inspection.

L I F E   It does sometimes seem like overkill. You've looked around the home. The realtor (seller's agent) has looked around. You asked questions and passed paperwork back and forth. Now, you have to pay another person to do more of the same? You don't have to. There is no law requiring an independent inspection of a home before it is sold. (The exception is termite or other pest-type inspections which are required in virtually all states.) Nope, you can save the $150 to $250 bucks. But, when the deal closes and you are the official owner of a home that, in one year, will need a new hot water heater, new wiring, and an expensive septic overhaul, you'll have only yourself to blame.

The independent inspection is important for two reasons. First, you want to know what you're in for. A recent national survey by a home inspection company found that two out of every five homes has serious defects requiring at least $500 in repairs. That doesn't count the long-term consequences of those problems if left undiscovered until they get much worse.

Second, the inspection is also a great bargaining tool. Let's say your inspector finds the home needs new plumbing in one bathroom. The cost: $475. This probably is not enough to kill the sale, but the seller doesn't know that. You can bargain with the seller to eat at least half the cost just to keep the deal alive. You'd be forced to make the repair eventually, but without the inspection, the seller wouldn't have been around to share financially in the experience.

The inspection requirement will be part of your official offer too. A little language that will allow you to get out of the deal if your inspector finds repair needs in excess of a mutually agreed amount.

- There is no law requiring the buyer or seller to pay for a home inspection, except for pest-related problems.

- Bargain with the seller to share the cost of repairs found necessary by the inspector.

- Your offer should include your right to an independent inspection and limit on repair costs.

MAKING AN OFFER TOO GOOD TO BE REFUSED

Dear Legal Edge:

We really like this one home we've looked at. Now the real estate agent says we need to make an offer. Is it too early to get nervous? I mean it's just an offer, right?

F.R.

L A W   An offer to buy a home becomes a binding contract if accepted by the seller. All terms of the offer become part of that contract.

L I F E   Take a deep breath. This is the single most important part of the home purchase process. What you do now will effect you physically, emotionally, spiritually, and financially for many, many years to come.

The offer starts with a real estate purchase contract, sometimes called a "deposit receipt." It can be a single page or as many as 12 pages. Read this document very carefully. The offer includes everything from the purchase price to the special features or fixtures you want to stay with the home when the seller moves. Everything you want. If your offer is accepted it will become the sales contract, but it is more likely you will work with the seller refining your original offer. Still, it's best to start with as specific an offer as possible.

Take a look at the Residential Purchase Agreement sample form on pages 131–135. It is one of the most complete you'll find. Don't worry if your offer doesn't include everything you see here. Ask the seller's real estate agent about anything you don't understand, remembering he or she is the seller's agent. You may feel more comfortable having your own people look over the offer, someone on your payroll. Don't forget the power you're giving the seller when you present the offer. He or she can accept it, immediately creating a binding contract. Better to make sure it's correct before you get into a deal you don't like.

- Be very specific about the details in your offer.

- Anticipate the things the seller might question.

- Have the offer reviewed by your agent or lawyer before presenting it to the seller.

OH WELL, COUNTER-OFFER

Dear Legal Edge:
We found this great house and we thought we put in a good offer, but the seller blew us off. We'd like to forget about it but the house is just what we want. Suggestions?
F.K.

L A W   When an offer is rejected, it dies. The seller has given up the right to accept the offer and may make a counter-offer.

L I F E   Okay, so your impossible-to-refuse offer was refused. Legally it was "rejected." The seller normally responds with a counter-offer, but not always. If you really want the home you

RESIDENTIAL PURCHASE AGREEMENT
(AND RECEIPT FOR DEPOSIT)
For Use With Single Family Residential Property — Attached or Detached

Date: _____, at _____, California,

Received From _____ ("Buyer"),

A Deposit Of _____ Dollars $ _____, toward the

Purchase Price Of _____ Dollars $ _____

For Purchase Of Property Situated In _____, County Of _____

California, Described As _____, ("Property").

1. **FINANCING:** Obtaining the loans below **is a contingency** of this Agreement. Buyer shall act diligently and in good faith to obtain the designated loans. Obtaining deposit, down payment and closing costs **is not a contingency.**

   A. **BUYER'S DEPOSIT** shall be held uncashed until Acceptance and then deposited within 3 **business days** after .. $ _____
      Acceptance or □ _____ □ _____ with Escrow Holder,
      □ into Broker's trust account, or □ _____, by □ Personal Check, □ Cashier's Check,
      □ Cash, or □ _____

   B. **INCREASED DEPOSIT** shall be deposited with _____ . $ _____
      within _____ **Days After Acceptance,** or □ _____

   C. **FIRST LOAN IN THE AMOUNT OF** .... $ _____
      NEW First Deed of Trust in favor of LENDER, encumbering the Property, securing a note payable at maximum
      interest of _____% fixed rate, or _____% initial adjustable rate with a maximum interest rate cap of
      _____%, balance due in _____ years. Buyer shall pay loan fees/points not to exceed _____.
      □ FHA □ VA: Seller shall pay (i) ___% discount points, (ii) other fees not allowed to be paid by Buyer,
      not to exceed $ _____, and (iii) the cost of lender required repairs not otherwise provided for in
      this Agreement, not to exceed $ _____.

   D. **ADDITIONAL FINANCING TERMS:** _____ . $ _____
      □ seller financing, (C.A.R. Form SFA-14); □ junior or assumed financing, (C.A.R. Form PAA-14, paragraph 5)

   E. **BALANCE OF PURCHASE PRICE** (not including costs of obtaining loans and other closing costs) to be deposited .. $ _____
      with escrow holder within sufficient time to close escrow.

   F. **TOTAL PURCHASE PRICE** .... $ _____

   G. **LOAN CONTINGENCY** shall remain in effect until the designated loans are funded (or □ _____ **Days After Acceptance,** by which time Buyer shall give Seller written notice of Buyer's election to cancel this Agreement if Buyer is unable to obtain the designated loans. If Buyer does not give Seller such notice, the contingency of obtaining the designated loans shall be removed by the method specified in paragraph 16B.)

   H. **LOAN APPLICATIONS; PREQUALIFICATION: For NEW financing,** within 5 (or □ _____) **Days After Acceptance,** Buyer shall provide Seller a letter from lender or mortgage loan broker stating that, based on a review of Buyer's written application and credit report, Buyer is prequalified for the NEW loan indicated above. If Buyer fails to provide such letter within that time, Seller may cancel this Agreement in writing.

   I. □ **APPRAISAL CONTINGENCY:** (If checked) This Agreement is contingent upon Property appraising at no less than the specified total purchase price. If there is a loan contingency, the appraisal contingency shall remain in effect until the loan contingency is removed, otherwise, the appraisal contingency shall be removed within 10 (or □ _____) **Days After Acceptance.**

   J. **ALL CASH OFFER:** If this is an all cash offer, Buyer shall, within 5 (or □ _____) **Days After Acceptance,** provide Seller written verification of sufficient funds to close this transaction. Seller may cancel this Agreement in writing within **5 Days After:** (i) time to provide verification expires, if Buyer fails to provide verification; or (ii) receipt of verification, if Seller reasonably disapproves it.

2. **ESCROW:** Close Of Escrow shall occur _____ **Days After Acceptance** (or □ on _____ (date). Buyer and Seller shall deliver signed escrow instructions consistent with this Agreement □ within _____ **Days After Acceptance,** □ at least _____ **Days** before Close Of Escrow, or □ _____. Seller shall deliver possession and occupancy of the Property to Buyer at _____ AM/PM, □ on the date of Close Of Escrow, □ no later than _____ **Days After** date of Close Of Escrow, or □ _____. Property shall be vacant, unless otherwise agreed in writing. If transfer of title and possession do not occur at the same time, Buyer and Seller are advised to (a) consult with their insurance advisors, and (b) enter into a written occupancy agreement. The omission from escrow instructions of any provision in this Agreement shall not constitute a waiver of that provision.

3. **OCCUPANCY:** Buyer □ does, □ does not, intend to occupy Property as Buyer's primary residence.

4. **ALLOCATION OF COSTS:** (Check boxes which apply. If needed, insert additional instructions in blank lines.)
   GOVERNMENTAL TRANSFER FEES:

   A. □ Buyer □ Seller shall pay County transfer tax or transfer fee. _____

   B. □ Buyer □ Seller shall pay City transfer tax or transfer fee. _____
   TITLE AND ESCROW COSTS:

   C. □ Buyer □ Seller shall pay for **owner's** title insurance policy, issued by _____ company.
      (Buyer shall pay for any title insurance policy insuring Buyer's **Lender,** unless otherwise agreed.)

   D. □ Buyer □ Seller shall pay escrow fee. _____ Escrow holder shall be _____.
   SEWER/SEPTIC/WELL COSTS:

   E. □ Buyer □ Seller shall pay for sewer connection, if required by Law prior to Close Of Escrow.

   F. □ Buyer □ Seller shall pay to have septic or private sewage disposal system inspected.

   G. □ Buyer □ Seller shall pay to have wells tested for water quality, potability, productivity and recovery rate.
   OTHER COSTS:

   H. □ Buyer □ Seller shall pay Homeowners' Association transfer fees.

   I. □ Buyer □ Seller shall pay Homeowners' Association document preparation fees.

   J. □ Buyer □ Seller shall pay for zone disclosure reports.

   K. □ Buyer □ Seller shall pay for Smoke Detector installation and/or Water Heater bracing. Seller, prior to close of escrow, shall provide Buyer a statement of compliance in accordance with state and local Law, unless exempt.

   L. □ Buyer □ Seller shall pay the cost of compliance with any other minimum mandatory government retrofit standards and inspections required as a condition of closing escrow under any Law.

   M. □ Buyer □ Seller shall pay the cost of a one-year home warranty plan, issued by _____ with the following optional coverage: _____. Policy cost not to exceed $ _____.
   PEST CONTROL REPORT:

   N. □ Buyer □ Seller shall pay for the **Pest Control Report** ("Report"), which, within the time specified in paragraph 16, shall be prepared by _____, a registered structural pest control company. _____

   O. (1) Buyer shall have the right to disapprove the Report as specified in paragraph 16, UNLESS any box in 4 O (2) is checked below
      OR (2) (Applies if any box is checked below)
      (a) □ Buyer □ Seller shall pay for work recommended to correct conditions described in the Report as **"Section 1."**
      (b) □ Buyer □ Seller shall pay for work recommended to correct conditions described in the Report as **"Section 2,"** unless waived by Buyer

Buyer and Seller acknowledge receipt of copy of this page, which constitutes Page 1 of _____ Pages.

Buyer's Initials (_____) (_____) Seller's Initials (_____) (_____)

— OFFICE USE ONLY —
Reviewed by Broker
or Designee _____
Date _____

REVISED 4/98

RESIDENTIAL PURCHASE AGREEMENT AND RECEIPT FOR DEPOSIT (RPA-14 PAGE 1 OF 5)

Property Address: _____ Date: _____

5. PEST CONTROL TERMS: If a Report is prepared pursuant to paragraph 4N:

    A. The Report shall cover the main building and attached structures and, if checked: ☐ detached garages and carports, ☐ detached decks, ☐ the following other structures on the Property: _____

    B. If Property is a unit in a condominium, planned development, or residential stock cooperative, the Report shall cover only the separate interest and any exclusive-use areas being transferred, and shall not cover common areas, unless otherwise agreed.

    C. If inspection of inaccessible areas is recommended in the Report, Buyer has the option, within 5 Days After receipt of the Report, either to accept and approve the Report by the method specified in paragraph 16B, or to request in writing that further inspection be made. If upon further inspection no infestation or infection is found in the inaccessible areas, the cost of the inspection, entry, and closing of those areas shall be paid for by Buyer. If upon further inspection infestation or infection is found in the inaccessible areas, the cost of inspection, entry, and closing of those areas shall be paid for by the party so designated in paragraph 4O(2)a. If no party is so designated, then cost shall be paid by Buyer.

    D. If no infestation or infection by wood destroying pests or organisms is found in the Report, or upon completion of required corrective work, a written Pest Control Certification shall be issued. Certification shall be issued prior to Close Of Escrow, unless otherwise agreed in writing.

    E. Inspections, corrective work and Pest Control Certification in this paragraph refers only to the presence or absence of wood destroying pests or organisms, and does not include the condition of roof coverings. Read paragraphs 9 and 1C concerning roof coverings.

    F. Nothing in paragraph 5 shall relieve Seller of the obligation to repair or replace shower pans and shower enclosures due to leaks, if required by paragraph 9B(3). Water test of shower pans on upper level units may not be performed unless the owners of property below the shower consent.

6. TRANSFER DISCLOSURE STATEMENT; NATURAL HAZARD DISCLOSURES; SUBSEQUENT DISCLOSURES; MELLO-ROOS NOTICE:

    A. Within the time specified in paragraph 16A(1), if required by law, a Real Estate Transfer Disclosure Statement ("TDS") and Natural Hazard Disclosure Statement ("NHD") (or substituted disclosure) shall be completed and delivered to Buyer, who shall return signed copies to Seller.

    B. In the event Seller, prior to Close Of Escrow, becomes aware of adverse conditions materially affecting the Property, or any material inaccuracy in disclosures, information, or representations previously provided to Buyer (including those made in a TDS) of which Buyer is otherwise unaware, Seller shall promptly provide a subsequent or amended disclosure in writing, covering those items, **except for those conditions and material inaccuracies disclosed in reports obtained by Buyer.**

    C. Seller shall (i) make a good faith effort to obtain a disclosure notice from any local agencies which levy a special tax on the Property pursuant to the Mello-Roos Community Facilities Act, and (ii) promptly deliver to Buyer any such notice made available by those agencies.

    D. If the TDS, the NHD (or substituted disclosure), the Mello-Roos disclosure notice, or a subsequent or amended disclosure is delivered to Buyer after the offer is signed, Buyer shall have the right to terminate this Agreement within **3 days** after delivery in person, or **5 days** after delivery by deposit in the mail, by giving written notice of termination to Seller or Seller's agent.

7. DISCLOSURES: Within the time specified in paragraph 16A(1), Seller, shall (i) if required by law, disclose if Property is located in any zone identified in 7A; (ii) if required by law, provide Buyer with the disclosures and other information identified in 7B, and, (iii) if applicable, take the actions specified in 7C. Buyer shall then, within the time specified in paragraph 16, investigate the disclosures and information, and other information provided to Buyer, and provide written notice to Seller of any item disapproved.

    A. ZONE DISCLOSURES: Special Flood Hazard Areas; Potential Flooding (Inundation) Areas; Very High Fire Hazard Zones; State Fire Responsibility Areas; Earthquake Fault Zones; Seismic Hazard Zones; or any other federal, state, or locally designated zone for which disclosure is required by Law.

    B. PROPERTY DISCLOSURES AND PUBLICATIONS: Lead-Based Paint Disclosures and pamphlet; Earthquake Guides (and disclosures), Environmental Hazards Booklet, and Energy Efficiency Booklet (when published).

    C. ☐ (If checked:) **CONDOMINIUM/COMMON INTEREST SUBDIVISION:** Property is a unit in a condominium, planned development, or other common interest subdivision. Seller shall request from the Homeowners' Association ("HOA"), and upon receipt provide to Buyer: copies of covenants, conditions, and restrictions; articles of incorporation, by-laws, and other governing documents; statement regarding limited enforceability of age restrictions, if applicable; copies of most current financial documents distributed; statement indicating current regular, special and emergency dues and assessments, any unpaid assessment, any additional amounts due from Seller or Property, any approved changes to regular, special or emergency dues or assessments; preliminary list of defects, if any; any written notice of settlement regarding common area defects; and any pending or anticipated claims or litigation by or against the HOA; any other documents required by Law; a statement containing the location and number of designated parking and storage spaces; and copies of the most recent 12 months of HOA minutes for regular and special meetings, if available.

    D. NOTICE OF VIOLATION: If, prior to Close Of Escrow, Seller receives notice or is made aware of any notice filed or issued against the Property, for violations of any Laws, Seller shall immediately notify Buyer in writing.

8. TITLE AND VESTING:

    A. Within the time specified in paragraph 16A, Buyer shall be provided a current preliminary (title) report (which is only an offer by the title insurer to issue a policy of title insurance, and may not contain every item affecting title). Buyer shall, within the time specified in paragraph 16A(2), provide written notice to Seller of any items reasonably disapproved.

    B. At Close Of Escrow, Buyer shall receive a grant deed conveying title (or, for stock cooperative or long-term lease, an assignment of stock certificate or of seller's interest), including oil, mineral and water rights, if currently owned by Seller. Title shall be subject to all encumbrances, easements, covenants, conditions, restrictions, rights, and other matters which are of record or disclosed to Buyer prior to Close Of Escrow, unless disapproved in writing by Buyer within the time specified in paragraph 16A(2). However, title shall not be subject to any liens against the Property, except for those specified in the Agreement. Buyer shall receive an ALTA-R owner's title insurance policy, if reasonably available. If not, Buyer shall receive a standard coverage owner's policy (e.g. CLTA or ALTA with regional exceptions). Title shall vest as designated in Buyer's escrow instructions. The title company, at Buyer's request, can provide information about availability, desirability, and cost of various title insurance coverages. THE MANNER OF TAKING TITLE MAY HAVE SIGNIFICANT LEGAL AND TAX CONSEQUENCES.

9. CONDITION OF PROPERTY:

    A. EXCEPT AS SPECIFIED IN THIS AGREEMENT, Property is sold "AS IS," WITHOUT WARRANTY, in its PRESENT physical condition.

    B. (IF CHECKED) SELLER WARRANTS THAT AT THE TIME POSSESSION IS MADE AVAILABLE TO BUYER:

      ☐ **(1)** Roof shall be free of leaks KNOWN to Seller or DISCOVERED during escrow.

      ☐ **(2)** Built-in appliances (including free-standing oven and range, if included), heating, air conditioning, electrical, mechanical, water, sewer, and pool/spa systems, if any, shall be repaired, if KNOWN by Seller to be inoperative or DISCOVERED to be so during escrow. (Well system is not warranted by this paragraph. Well system is covered by paragraphs 4G, 12 and 16.)

      ☐ **(3)** Plumbing systems, shower pans, and shower enclosures shall be free of leaks KNOWN to Seller or DISCOVERED during escrow.

      ☐ **(4)** All fire safety and structural defects in chimneys and fireplaces KNOWN to Seller or DISCOVERED during escrow shall be repaired.

      ☐ **(5)** Septic system, if any, shall be repaired, if KNOWN by Seller to be inoperative, or DISCOVERED to be so during escrow.

      ☐ **(6)** All broken or cracked glass, torn existing window and door screens, and multi-pane windows with broken seals, shall be replaced.

      ☐ **(7)** All debris and all personal property not included in the sale shall be removed.

      ☐ **(8)** _____

    C. PROPERTY MAINTENANCE: Unless otherwise agreed, Property, including pool, spa, landscaping and grounds, is to be maintained in substantially the same condition as on the date of Acceptance.

    D. INSPECTIONS AND DISCLOSURES: Items discovered in Buyer's Inspections which are not covered by paragraph 9B, shall be governed by the procedure in paragraphs 12 and 16. Buyer retains the right to disapprove the condition of the Property based upon items discovered in Buyer's Inspections. Disclosures in the TDS and items discovered in Buyer's Inspections do NOT eliminate Seller's obligations under paragraph 9B, unless specifically agreed in writing. WHETHER OR NOT SELLER WARRANTS ANY ASPECT OF THE PROPERTY, SELLER IS OBLIGATED TO DISCLOSE KNOWN MATERIAL FACTS, AND TO MAKE OTHER DISCLOSURES REQUIRED BY LAW

Buyer and Seller acknowledge receipt of copy of this page, which constitutes Page 2 of _____ Pages.

Buyer's Initials (_____) (_____)   Seller's Initials (_____) (_____)

REVISED 4/98

RESIDENTIAL PURCHASE AGREEMENT AND RECEIPT FOR DEPOSIT (RPA-14 PAGE 2 OF 5)

Property Address: _____ **Date:** _____

10. **FIXTURES:** All EXISTING fixtures and fittings that are attached to the Property, or for which special openings have been made, are INCLUDED IN THE PURCHASE PRICE (unless excluded below), and shall be transferred free of liens and "AS IS," unless specifically warranted. Fixtures shall include, but are not limited to, existing electrical, mechanical, lighting, plumbing and heating fixtures, fireplace inserts, solar systems, built-in appliances, window and door screens, awnings, shutters, window coverings, attached floor coverings, television antennas, satellite dishes and related equipment, private integrated telephone systems, air coolers/conditioners, pool/spa equipment, garage door openers/remote controls, attached fireplace equipment, mailbox, in-ground landscaping, including trees/shrubs, and (if owned by Seller) water softeners, water purifiers and security systems/alarms, and _____.
    FIXTURES EXCLUDED: _____
11. **PERSONAL PROPERTY:** The following items of personal property, free of liens and "AS IS," unless specifically warranted, are INCLUDED IN THE PURCHASE PRICE: _____
12. **BUYER'S INVESTIGATION OF PROPERTY CONDITION:** Buyer's Acceptance of the condition of the Property is a contingency of this Agreement, as specified in this paragraph and paragraph 16. Buyer shall have the right, at Buyer's expense, to conduct inspections, investigations, tests, surveys, and other studies ("Inspections"), including the right to inspect for lead-based paint and other lead hazards. No Inspections shall be made by any governmental building or zoning inspector, or government employee, without Seller's prior written consent, unless required by Law. Property improvements may not be built according to codes or in compliance with current Law, or have had permits issued. Buyer shall, within the time specified in Paragraph 16A(2), complete these Inspections and notify Seller in writing of any items reasonably disapproved. Seller shall make Property available for all Inspections. Buyer shall: keep Property free and clear of liens; indemnify and hold Seller harmless from all liability, claims, demands, damages and costs; and repair all damages arising from Inspections. Buyer shall carry, or Buyer shall require anyone acting on Buyer's behalf to carry, policies of liability, worker's compensation, and other applicable insurance, defending and protecting Seller from liability for any injuries to persons or property occurring during any work done on the Property at Buyer's direction, prior to Close Of Escrow. Seller is advised that certain protections may be afforded Seller by recording a notice of non-responsibility for work done on the Property at Buyer's direction. At Seller's request, Buyer shall give Seller, at no cost, complete copies of all Inspection reports obtained by Buyer concerning the Property. Seller shall have water, gas, and electricity on for Buyer's Inspections, and through the date possession is made available to Buyer.
13. **FINAL WALK-THROUGH; VERIFICATION OF CONDITION:** Buyer shall have the right to make a final inspection of the Property within 5 (or ☐ _____) Days prior to Close Of Escrow, NOT AS A CONTINGENCY OF THE SALE, but solely to confirm that Repairs have been completed as agreed in writing, and that Seller has complied with Seller's other obligations.
14. **PRORATIONS AND PROPERTY TAXES:** Unless otherwise agreed in writing, real property taxes and assessments, interest, rents, HOA regular, special, and emergency dues and assessments imposed prior to Close Of Escrow, premiums on insurance assumed by Buyer, payments on bonds and assessments assumed by Buyer, and payments on Mello-Roos and other Special Assessment District bonds and assessments which are now a lien shall be PAID CURRENT and prorated between Buyer and Seller as of Close Of Escrow. Prorated payments on Mello-Roos and other Special Assessment District bonds and assessments and HOA special assessments that are now a lien but not yet due, shall be assumed by Buyer WITHOUT CREDIT toward the purchase price. Property will be reassessed upon change of ownership. Any supplemental tax bills shall be paid as follows: **(1)** For periods after Close Of Escrow, by Buyer; and, **(2)** For periods prior to Close Of Escrow, by Seller. TAX BILLS ISSUED AFTER CLOSE OF ESCROW SHALL BE HANDLED DIRECTLY BETWEEN BUYER AND SELLER. Exceptions: _____
    _____

15. **SALE OF BUYER'S PROPERTY:**
    A. This Agreement is NOT contingent upon the sale of Buyer's property, unless paragraph 15B is checked.
    OR B. ☐ (If checked) This Agreement IS CONTINGENT on the Close Of Escrow of Buyer's property, described as (address) _____
    _____ ("Buyer's Property"), which is
    (if checked) ☐ listed for sale with _____ Company, and/or
    (if checked) ☐ in Escrow No. _____ with _____ Escrow Holder, scheduled to
    Close Escrow on _____ (date). Buyer shall deliver to Seller, within **5 Days** After Seller's request, a copy of the contract for the sale of Buyer's Property, escrow instructions, and all amendments and modifications thereto. If Buyer's Property does not close escrow by the date specified for Close Of Escrow in this paragraph, then either Seller or Buyer may cancel this Agreement in writing.
    After Acceptance:
    (1) (Applies UNLESS (2) is checked): Seller SHALL have the right to continue to offer the Property for sale. If Seller accepts another written offer, Seller shall give Buyer written notice to **(i)** remove this contingency in writing, **(ii)** provide written verification of sufficient funds to close escrow on this sale without the sale of Buyer's Property, and **(iii)** comply with the following additional requirement(s) _____
    _____
    If Buyer fails to complete those actions within **72 (or ☐ _____) hours** After receipt of such notice, Seller may cancel this Agreement in writing.
    OR ☐ (2) (APPLIES ONLY IF CHECKED): Seller SHALL NOT have the right to continue to offer the Property for sale, except for back-up offers.
16. **TIME PERIODS/DISAPPROVAL RIGHTS/REMOVAL OF CONTINGENCIES/CANCELLATION RIGHTS:**
    A. TIME PERIODS: The following time periods shall apply, unless changed by mutual written agreement:
    (1) SELLER HAS: 5 (or ☐ _____) Days After Acceptance to, as applicable, order, request or complete, and **2 Days** After receipt (or completion) to provide to Buyer all reports, disclosures, and information for which Seller is responsible under paragraphs 4, 6, 7, and 8.
    (2) BUYER HAS: (a) 10 (or ☐ _____) Days After Acceptance to complete all Inspections, investigations and review of reports and other applicable information for which Buyer is responsible,(including Inspections for lead-based paint and other lead hazards under paragraph 12), with an additional **7 Days** to complete geologic Inspections. WITHIN THIS TIME, Buyer must either disapprove in writing any items, (including, if applicable, the pest control Report under paragraph 4O(1)) which are unacceptable to Buyer, or remove any contingency or disapproval right associated with that item by the active or passive method, as specified below; **(b) 5 (or ☐ _____) Days** After receipt of **(i)** each of the items in paragraph 16A(1); and, **(ii)** notice of code and legal violations under paragraph 7D, to either disapprove in writing any items which are unacceptable to Buyer or to remove any contingency or disapproval right associated with that item, by the active or passive method, as specified below.
    (3) SELLER'S RESPONSE TO BUYER'S DISAPPROVALS: Seller shall have **5 (or ☐ _____) Days** After receipt of Buyer's written notice of items reasonably disapproved, to respond in writing. If Seller refuses or is unable to make repairs to, or correct, any items reasonably disapproved by Buyer, or if Seller does not respond within the time period specified, Buyer shall have **5 (or ☐ _____) Days** After receipt of Seller's response, or after the expiration of the time for Seller to respond, whichever occurs first, to cancel this Agreement in writing.
    B. ACTIVE OR PASSIVE REMOVAL OF BUYER'S CONTINGENCIES:
    (1) ☐ ACTIVE METHOD (APPLIES IF CHECKED): If Buyer does not give Seller written notice of items reasonably disapproved, removal of contingencies or disapproval right, or notice of cancellation within the time periods specified, Seller shall have the right to cancel this Agreement by giving written notice to Buyer.
    (2) PASSIVE METHOD (Applies UNLESS Active Method is checked): If Buyer does not give Seller written notice of items reasonably disapproved, of removal of contingencies or disapproval right, or notice of cancellation within the time periods specified, Buyer shall be deemed to have removed and waived any contingency or disapproval right, or the right to cancel, associated with that item.
    C. EFFECT OF CONTINGENCY REMOVAL: If Buyer removes any contingency or cancellation right by the active or passive method, as applicable, Buyer conclusively shall be deemed to have: **(1)** Completed all Inspections, investigations, and review of reports and other applicable information and disclosures pertaining to that contingency or cancellation right; **(2)** Elected to proceed with the transaction; and, **(3)** Assumed all liability, responsibility, and expense for repairs or corrections pertaining to that contingency or cancellation right, or for inability to obtain financing if the contingency pertains to financing, except for items which Seller has agreed in writing to repair or correct.

Buyer and Seller acknowledge receipt of copy of this page, which constitutes Page 3 of _____ Pages.
Buyer's Initials (_____) (_____) Seller's Initials (_____) (_____)

REVISED 4/98

RESIDENTIAL PURCHASE AGREEMENT AND RECEIPT FOR DEPOSIT (RPA-14 PAGE 3 OF 5)

Property Address: _____ Date: _____

D. CANCELLATION OF SALE/ESCROW; RETURN OF DEPOSITS: If Buyer or Seller gives written NOTICE OF CANCELLATION pursuant to rights duly exercised under the terms of this Agreement, Buyer and Seller agree to sign mutual instructions to cancel the sale and escrow and release deposits, less fees and costs, to the party entitled to the funds. Fees and costs may be payable to service providers and vendors for services and products provided during escrow. Release of funds will require mutual, signed release instructions from both Buyer and Seller, judicial decision, or arbitration award. **A party may be subject to a civil penalty of up to $1,000 for refusal to sign such instructions, if no good faith dispute exists as to who is entitled to the deposited funds** (Civil Code §1057.3).

17. REPAIRS: Repairs under this Agreement shall be completed prior to Close Of Escrow, unless otherwise agreed in writing. Work to be performed at Seller's expense may be performed by Seller or through others, provided that work complies with applicable laws, including governmental permit, inspection, and approval requirements. Repairs shall be performed in a skillful manner with materials of quality comparable to existing materials. It is understood that exact restoration of appearance or cosmetic items following all Repairs may not be possible.

18. WITHHOLDING TAXES: Seller and Buyer agree to execute and deliver any instrument, affidavit, statement, or instruction reasonably necessary to comply with federal (FIRPTA) and California withholding Laws, if required (such as C.A.R. Forms AS-11 and AB-11).

19. KEYS: At the time possession is made available to Buyer, Seller shall provide keys and/or means to operate all Property locks, mailboxes, security systems, alarms, and garage door openers. If the Property is a unit in a condominium or subdivision, Buyer may be required to pay a deposit to the HOA to obtain keys to accessible HOA facilities.

20. LIQUIDATED DAMAGES: If Buyer fails to complete this purchase by reason of any default of Buyer, Seller shall retain, as liquidated damages for breach of contract, the deposit actually paid. However, if the Property is a dwelling with no more than four units, one of which Buyer intends to occupy, then the amount retained shall be no more than 3% of the purchase price. Any excess shall be returned to Buyer. Buyer and Seller shall also sign a separate liquidated damages provision for any increased deposit. (C.A.R. Form RID-11 shall fulfill this requirement.) Buyer's Initials _____/_____   Seller's Initials _____/_____

21. DISPUTE RESOLUTION:

A. MEDIATION: Buyer and Seller agree to mediate any dispute or claim arising between them out of this Agreement, or any resulting transaction, before resorting to arbitration or court action, subject to paragraphs 21C and D below. Mediation fees, if any, shall be divided equally among the parties involved. If any party commences an action based on a dispute or claim to which this paragraph applies, without first attempting to resolve the matter through mediation, then that party shall not be entitled to recover attorney's fees, even if they would otherwise be available to that party in any such action. THIS MEDIATION PROVISION APPLIES WHETHER OR NOT THE ARBITRATION PROVISION IS INITIALED.

B. ARBITRATION OF DISPUTES: Buyer and Seller agree that any dispute or claim in Law or equity arising between them out of this Agreement or any resulting transaction, which is not settled through mediation, shall be decided by neutral, binding arbitration, subject to paragraphs 21C and D below. The arbitrator shall be a retired judge or justice, or an attorney with at least 5 years of residential real estate Law experience, unless the parties mutually agree to a different arbitrator, who shall render an award in accordance with substantive California Law. In all other respects, the arbitration shall be conducted in accordance with Part III, Title 9 of the California Code of Civil Procedure. Judgment upon the award of the arbitrator(s) may be entered in any court having jurisdiction. The parties shall have the right to discovery in accordance with Code of Civil Procedure §1283.05.

"NOTICE: BY INITIALING IN THE SPACE BELOW YOU ARE AGREEING TO HAVE ANY DISPUTE ARISING OUT OF THE MATTERS INCLUDED IN THE 'ARBITRATION OF DISPUTES' PROVISION DECIDED BY NEUTRAL ARBITRATION AS PROVIDED BY CALIFORNIA LAW AND YOU ARE GIVING UP ANY RIGHTS YOU MIGHT POSSESS TO HAVE THE DISPUTE LITIGATED IN A COURT OR JURY TRIAL. BY INITIALING IN THE SPACE BELOW YOU ARE GIVING UP YOUR JUDICIAL RIGHTS TO DISCOVERY AND APPEAL, UNLESS THOSE RIGHTS ARE SPECIFICALLY INCLUDED IN THE 'ARBITRATION OF DISPUTES' PROVISION. IF YOU REFUSE TO SUBMIT TO ARBITRATION AFTER AGREEING TO THIS PROVISION, YOU MAY BE COMPELLED TO ARBITRATE UNDER THE AUTHORITY OF THE CALIFORNIA CODE OF CIVIL PROCEDURE. YOUR AGREEMENT TO THIS ARBITRATION PROVISION IS VOLUNTARY."

"WE HAVE READ AND UNDERSTAND THE FOREGOING AND AGREE TO SUBMIT DISPUTES ARISING OUT OF THE MATTERS INCLUDED IN THE 'ARBITRATION OF DISPUTES' PROVISION TO NEUTRAL ARBITRATION."   Buyer's Initials _____/_____   Seller's Initials _____/_____

C. EXCLUSIONS FROM MEDIATION AND ARBITRATION: The following matters are excluded from Mediation and Arbitration: (a) A judicial or non-judicial foreclosure or other action or proceeding to enforce a deed of trust, mortgage, or installment land sale contract as defined in Civil Code §2985; (b) An unlawful detainer action; (c) The filing or enforcement of a mechanic's lien; (d) Any matter which is within the jurisdiction of a probate, small claims, or bankruptcy court; and (e) An action for bodily injury or wrongful death, or for latent or patent defects to which Code of Civil Procedure §337.1 or §337.15 applies. The filing of a court action to enable the recording of a notice of pending action, for order of attachment, receivership, injunction, or other provisional remedies, shall not constitute a violation of the mediation and arbitration provisions.

D. BROKERS: Buyer and Seller agree to mediate and arbitrate disputes or claims involving either or both Brokers, provided either or both Brokers shall have agreed to such mediation or arbitration, prior to or within a reasonable time after the dispute or claim is presented to Brokers. Any election by either or both Brokers to participate in mediation or arbitration shall not result in Brokers being deemed parties to the Agreement.

22. DEFINITIONS: As used in this Agreement:

A. "Acceptance" means the time the offer or final counter offer is accepted in writing by the other party, in accordance with this Agreement or the terms of the final counter offer.

B. "Agreement" means the terms and conditions of this Residential Purchase Agreement and any counter offer.

C. "Days" means calendar days, unless otherwise required by Law.

D. "Days After . ." means the specified number of calendar days after the occurrence of the event specified, not counting the calendar date on which the specified event occurs.

E. "Close Of Escrow" means the date the grant deed, or other evidence of transfer of title, is recorded.

F. "Law" means any law, code, statute, ordinance, regulation, rule, which is adopted by a controlling city, county, state or federal legislative or judicial body or agency.

G. "Repairs" means any repairs, alterations, replacements, or modifications, (including pest control work) of the Property.

H. "Pest Control Certification" means a written statement made by a registered structural pest control company that on the date of inspection or re-inspection, the Property is "free" or is "now free" of "evidence of active infestation in the visible and accessible areas".

I. Section 1 means infestation or infection which is evident. **Section 2** means present conditions likely to lead to infestation or infection.

J. Singular and Plural forms each include the other, when appropriate.

K. C.A.R. Form means the specific form referenced, or another comparable form agreed to by the parties.

23. MULTIPLE LISTING SERVICE ("MLS"): Brokers are authorized to report the terms of this transaction to any MLS, to be published and disseminated to persons and entities authorized to use the information, on terms approved by the MLS.

Buyer and Seller acknowledge receipt of copy of this page, which constitutes Page 4 of _____ Pages.
Buyer's Initials (_____) (_____) Seller's Initials (_____) (_____)

REVISED 4/98

RESIDENTIAL PURCHASE AGREEMENT AND RECEIPT FOR DEPOSIT (RPA-14 PAGE 4 OF 5)

Property Address: _____ Date: _____

24. **EQUAL HOUSING OPPORTUNITY:** The Property is sold in compliance with federal, state, and local anti-discrimination Laws.

25. **ATTORNEY'S FEES:** In any action, proceeding, or arbitration between Buyer and Seller arising out of this Agreement, the prevailing Buyer or Seller shall be entitled to reasonable attorney's fees and costs from the non-prevailing Buyer or Seller, except as provided in paragraph 21A.

26. **SELECTION OF SERVICE PROVIDERS:** If Brokers give Buyer or Seller referrals to persons, vendors, or service or product providers ("Providers"), Brokers do not guarantee the performance of any of those Providers. Buyer and Seller may select ANY Providers of their own choosing.

27. **TIME OF ESSENCE; ENTIRE CONTRACT; CHANGES:** Time is of the essence. All understandings between the parties are incorporated in this Agreement. Its terms are intended by the parties as a final, complete, and exclusive expression of their agreement with respect to its subject matter, and may not be contradicted by evidence of any prior agreement or contemporaneous oral agreement. **This Agreement may not be extended, amended, modified, altered, or changed, except in writing signed by Buyer and Seller.**

28. **OTHER TERMS AND CONDITIONS,** including **ATTACHED SUPPLEMENTS:**
    ☑ Buyer Inspection Advisory (C.A.R. Form BIA-14) _____
    ☐ Purchase Agreement Addendum (C.A.R. Form PAA-14 paragraph numbers: _____)
    _____
    _____
    _____

29. **AGENCY CONFIRMATION:** The following agency relationships are hereby confirmed for this transaction:
    Listing Agent: _____ (Print Firm Name) is the agent of (check one):
    ☐ the Seller exclusively; or ☐ both the Buyer and Seller.
    Selling Agent: _____ (Print Firm Name) (if not same as Listing Agent) is the agent of (check one):
    ☐ the Buyer exclusively; or ☐ the Seller exclusively; or ☐ both the Buyer and Seller.
    Real Estate Brokers are not parties to the Agreement between Buyer and Seller.

30. **OFFER:** This is an offer to purchase the Property on the above terms and conditions. All paragraphs with spaces for initials by Buyer and Seller are incorporated in this Agreement only if initialed by all parties. If at least one but not all parties initial, a counter offer is required until agreement is reached. Unless Acceptance of Offer is signed by Seller, and a signed copy delivered in person, by mail, or facsimile, and personally received by Buyer, or by _____, who is authorized to receive it, by (date) _____, at _____ AM/PM, the offer shall be deemed revoked and the deposit shall be returned. Buyer has read and acknowledges receipt of a copy of the offer and agrees to the above confirmation of agency relationships. If this offer is accepted and Buyer subsequently defaults, Buyer may be responsible for payment of Brokers' compensation. This Agreement and any supplement, addendum, or modification, including any photocopy or facsimile, may be signed in two or more counterparts, all of which shall constitute one and the same writing.

Buyer and Seller acknowledge and agree that Brokers: (a) Do not decide what price Buyer should pay or Seller should accept; (b) Do not guarantee the condition of the Property; (c) Shall not be responsible for defects that are not known to Broker(s) and are not visually observable in reasonably accessible areas of the Property; (d) Do not guarantee the performance or Repairs of others who have provided services or products to Buyer or Seller; (e) Cannot identify Property boundary lines; (f) Cannot verify inspection reports, square footage or representations of others; (g) Cannot provide legal or tax advice; (h) Will not provide other advice or information that exceeds the knowledge, education and experience required to obtain a real estate license. Buyer and Seller agree that they will seek legal, tax, insurance, and other desired assistance from appropriate professionals.

BUYER _____ BUYER _____

31. **BROKER COMPENSATION:** Seller agrees to pay compensation for services as follows:
    _____, to _____, Broker, and
    _____, to _____, Broker,
    payable: **(a)** On recordation of the deed or other evidence of title; or **(b)** If completion of sale is prevented by default of Seller, upon Seller's default; or, **(c)** If completion of sale is prevented by default of Buyer, only if and when Seller collects damages from Buyer, by suit or otherwise, and then in an amount equal to one-half of the damages recovered, but not to exceed the above compensation, after first deducting title and escrow expenses and the expenses of collection, if any. Seller hereby irrevocably assigns to Brokers such compensation from Seller's proceeds, and irrevocably instructs Escrow Holder to disburse those funds to Brokers at close of escrow. Commission instructions can be amended or revoked only with the written consent of Brokers. In any action, proceeding or arbitration relating to the payment of such compensation, the prevailing party shall be entitled to reasonable attorney's fees and costs, except as provided in paragraph 21A.

32. **ACCEPTANCE OF OFFER:** Seller warrants that Seller is the owner of this Property, or has the authority to execute this Agreement. Seller accepts the above offer, agrees to sell the Property on the above terms and conditions, and agrees to the above confirmation of agency relationships. Seller has read and acknowledges receipt of a copy of this Agreement, and authorizes Broker to deliver a signed copy to Buyer.

If checked: ☐ SUBJECT TO ATTACHED COUNTER OFFER, DATED _____.

SELLER _____ Date _____

SELLER _____ Date _____

(____/____) **ACKNOWLEDGMENT OF RECEIPT:** Buyer or authorized agent acknowledges receipt of signed Acceptance on (date) _____,
(Initials) ____ AM/PM.

Agency relationships are confirmed as above. Real Estate Brokers are not parties to the Agreement between Buyer and Seller.
Receipt for deposit is acknowledged.
Real Estate Broker (Selling Firm Name) _____ By _____ Date _____
Address _____ Telephone _____ Fax _____
Real Estate Broker (Listing Firm Name) _____ By _____ Date _____
Address _____ Telephone _____ Fax _____

REVISED 4/98

Page 5 of _____ Pages.

OFFICE USE ONLY
Reviewed by Broker
or Designee _____
Date _____

EQUAL HOUSING OPPORTUNITY

RESIDENTIAL PURCHASE AGREEMENT AND RECEIPT FOR DEPOSIT (RPA-14 PAGE 5 OF 5)

may have to come up with a better offer. How badly do you want the home?

Here's one rule that you should never break: Don't bid against yourself. Let's say you offer $100,000 for the home but the offer is rejected and the seller makes no counter-offer. You really, really, really want this house, so you make a new offer of $110,000. You've just bid against yourself. The seller has not contributed to the compromise process and now knows you want this home and is less likely to bar-  gain. But, Mike, we really, really, really want this home. Okay, so bid against yourself if you must. Just realize you are putting your-self in a very weak bargaining position. Accept that, make a deal, and don't look back.

On the other hand, it is the rare seller, especially if represented by a real estate agent, who simply blows off an offer. Generally, a seller will consider and respond to most offers with a counter-offer. You can help control the seller's counter-offer. Your original offer will give the seller room to move toward the price and con-ditions you will accept. That is not to say you should "low-ball" the seller. Just stay on the low end of reasonable. Say the asking price is $125,000. If the home is worth $110,000 to you, based on your review of other homes, other neighborhoods, and what your lender thinks you can afford, your original offer of $100,000 is on the low end of reasonable. It's 20 percent off the asking price. Assuming there aren't a bunch of issues about things like who gets the drapes or the mirror ball in the master bedroom, a reasonable counter-offer from the seller would be in the $110,000 to $115,000 range. Now you're getting close to the number you like.

This offer/counter-offer dance may go back and forth a few times before one of two things happens: You agree to the deal or you part company grumbling about how unreasonable the other person was. Let it go. This is a major negotiation for everyone.

Don't get emotional. Stick to the business of buying a home and leave the rest for your anger-management class.

- If your original offer is rejected, do not bid against yourself by making another offer.

- Ask the seller to make a counter-offer.

- Help control the seller's counter-offer by leaving room to raise your original offer to meet the lowered asking price.

THE OFFER BECOMES A CONTRACT

Dear Legal Edge Man:

This home we're buying has lots in it that I like. There's a pool table, big screen TV, and some great tools in the garage. My wife says we can't include those in our offer. Can we?

G.H.

L A W   An offer must identify everything you want included in the purchase price of the home. The deposit, down payment, and special features or fixtures should be itemized to avoid argument over what is being bought and sold.

L I F E   Whether your spouse lets you include unattached fixtures or features (toys or goodies) in your offer is one thing, but do it unless you like surprises. You buy the home thinking it includes the extras you saw while shopping, but on move-in day you have no drapes, no fancy lights and the pool table is gone.

Many a home sale has gone south because neither the buyer nor seller made it clear what was and what was not included in the offer. That is why you will see plenty of blank space on an offer or real estate contract, to list these knick-knacks, gewgaws, and attatchments. You don't want to make an offer on the "home" alone and then start piece-mealing the other items. After all, this is not an auction. You're also going to get a better price by lumping everything into one big number.

This strategy does not mean that you won't end up haggling with the seller over odds and ends. You might. But by putting all extras in your offer, generally those items not attached or easily removable (like drapes, fancy light fixtures, or ceiling fans), you make it clear from the start exactly what you want and the deal won't die from massive misunderstanding.

- Include in your offer all items you want to buy as part of the home sale agreement.

- Normally, items permanently attached to the house are considered part of the home and don't need to be itemized.

- Do not price fixtures separately. Make one lump sum offer.

IS IT TOO LATE TO GET OUT OF THE DEAL?

Dear Legal Edge:

We love this home and we know we can afford it, but what happens if the bank says we can't? We've already signed the contract to buy.

A.Y.

L A W   Every contract to buy a home includes "conditions" which must be fulfilled before the seller or buyer is legally obligated to complete the deal.

L I F E   The day you sign the contract agreeing to buy a home is high up there on the sweaty palms scale. But, fear not, for you will include in your contract many conditions allowing you or the seller to escape if a problem comes up. A condition is an event that must happen before a contract becomes binding, legally enforceable. The most common condition involves money. The buyer is not obligated to go through with the sale unless he get funds from a lender, the sale of another home, or a rich uncle. That doesn't mean you can change your mind for other reasons and then claim no bank will give you the dough. Your inability to get funding must be legit.

One important note on the issue of funding. Working with the bank or other lenders can be intimidating and, yes, they can make you feel small and insignificant. But, don't give up if your loan application is denied. Try this scenario. A couple goes to the bank for a home loan. She recently started a new job which, at first glance, appears to pay less than the bank needs to approve the loan. The husband makes a relatively steady income, but both incomes need to be considered to get this loan. They are denied. Undaunted, the couple creates a graph showing the rapid increase in the wife's earnings over the first six months of her new job. She gets a letter from her boss explaining the nature of her business and anticipated future growth. The couple presents this information to the bank and after a second look . . . bingo . . . the bank gives them the loan. They get their home. The point is this: make the effort to convince the lender you have the ability and desire to uphold your financial commitment.

Financing is just one type of condition. Others include passing certain inspections, or setting limits on the cost of any repairs. An example of this kind of condition is: "If the roof needs more than $2000 in repairs, buyer shall not be obligated to complete the home purchase." You can set up conditions for anything, as long as both sides agree to the condition. But make sure it is spelled out in the offer or contract.

- A condition is an event in the contract that must happen before the home sale is binding.

- Include in your contract all conditions that must happen, such as financing, passed inspections, or zoning requirements.

WE'VE JUST CHANGED OUR MINDS

Dear Legal Edge:
I think we rushed into this too fast. We found a home, made an offer

and the lady accepted. Now the paperwork is being processed and we just found a better deal. Can you help?

C.W.

L A W   If all conditions for the home sale are fulfilled, both buyer and seller are legally obligated to complete the sale or pay a penalty for violating the contract.

L I F E   Flash! You are not the first to get deep into the home sale experience and change your mind. The only question is, "How badly do you want out and at what cost?" When you made your offer you probably included a deposit, a relatively small amount of dough called "earnest money." The actual deposit amount depends on the price of the home and your negotiation with the seller, reckon $1,000 to $5,000. This is basically showing the seller that you are serious about buying her home. If you bail on the deal without a good legal reason—like you couldn't get financing, repairs costing more than agreed or some other condition listed in the contract—you will lose your deposit. If that's all you lose the decision to bolt may be simple. But watch out for other penalties.

Some home sale contracts include "liquidated damages" clauses. These rules allow the jilted seller to sue you for amounts above and beyond your deposit. The amount can vary dramatically. Do your best to limit any liquidated damages to the amount of your deposit. Or, refuse to sign any contract that includes such a provision.

One other possible problem. Because real estate is so unique, the courts have decided that a seller or buyer can sue to make the deal happen even if one person wants to walk away. It is extreme, but this is called "specific performance," and the rule allows the seller go to court to force you to buy his home. If the seller can prove his home is so special, so unique that it would be difficult or impossible to get another buyer, a judge can say, "Congratulations, you've just bought a home." Once again, try to wipe out this possibility early in the contract stage by limiting what the seller can do if you take a hike. Let her have the deposit money and move on. Then try not to be so impulsive next time.

- Find out what penalties you must pay if you just change your mind and walk away from a home sale agreement.

- Before signing, try to limit any penalty to the amount of your deposit or "earnest money."

- Put up as small a deposit as the seller will allow.

IT'S A DEAL—NOW WHAT?

Dear Mr. Bryant:

I feel like I've just given birth. My wife and I finally found the home we are going to buy. All the paperwork is in and we are just waiting for the bank to get theirs together. Is there anything we need to do during this waiting time?

D.P.

L A W   Once you have a signed contract to buy or sell a home, a neutral third party or company called an "escrow agent," gathers all the information and assures that all conditions have been met before the property changes hands. Escrow is the period of time in which all money and legal documents are collected before being distributed to the parties as ownership is passed from seller to buyer.

L I F E   Once an offer is accepted, the contract is signed by both the seller and the buyer, and all conditions have been met, you have a legally binding agreement. Now it is important for you to stay involved with the escrow company or another neutral person handling the paperwork. This person is collecting information from the bank and the inspection people, and checking title documents.

Escrow is "opened." Escrow is really just a fancy way of saying someone will collect and hold all the things needed to complete the sale. It can be any neutral third person, someone not involved on the buyer's side or the seller's. Escrow is any person or company used to do the job that leads to closing the deal.

From this escrow person you will get "escrow instructions." This is a list of things the seller and buyer must do. (See the Escrow Instructions sample form on pages 143–146). Insurance, inspections, how much money is being held as a deposit, lender info. It's a great checklist to help you keep up with the home buying process. Take a look at the sample escrow instructions. Your instructions may not be as complete, but should still include the basic duties of the buyer and seller.

"Closing" happens when all paperwork is checked and signed and the government folks at city hall or the county can "record" the new owner of the property on title papers. This whole process can take some time. When you first open escrow, you will be told the estimated number of days before closing. In most areas a 45- to 60-day escrow is average. You may want a shorter escrow period if you or the seller needs to move fast. Maybe she has a new home to move into or is already paying for two houses and wants to stop that cash drain. You may want a longer escrow period. Perhaps you're moving into town from another area to start a job in ninety days. So, you don't want to own the home too soon. There are lots of reasons to change the length of escrow. Don't just nod your head when you're given an estimated number of days. Ask for an escrow period that works for you.

So, a month or two of twiddling your thumbs, huh? Nope. You're on the phone every day. To the escrow or title insurance company about getting the policy report. The sooner you find out about title problems, the more quickly they get fixed. On the phone to the inspection people. If you need to deal with pests or repairs before closing, you'd better get people going. On the phone to the bank or lender. "Hey, can I do anything to help you get your part of this deal done?" Your approach should always be, "How can I help you do what you need to do?" Not, "Hurry up and help me."

ESCROW INSTRUCTIONS

TO:
ADDRESS:

ESCROW NO.:
DATE:

_____

_____HEREINAFTER REFERRED TO AS "SELLER" AND_____

_____HEREINAFTER REFERRED TO AS "BUYER"

DO HEREBY INSTRUCT   AS FOLLOWS:

1.   To issue your current form of Preliminary Title Report on the real property known as:

_____

_____

2.   It is agreed by and between the parties hereto that said subject property above described is being purchased by BUYER and sold by SELLER under the following terms and conditions:

    a. SALE PRICE $ _____

    b. DOWN PAYMENT $ _____

    c. NEW FINANCING TO BE OBTAINED FROM: _____

_____$ _____

    d. EXISTING LOAN WITH: _____

_____$ _____

    e. NEW PURCHASE MONEY NOTE AND DEED OF TRUST IN FAVOR OF: ___

_____$ _____

ADDITIONAL TERMS _____

_____

_____

_____

3. In connection herewith, the following are to be submitted to escrow by the BUYER:
   ( ) Check in the amount of $_____as earnest money to be
      applied toward the down payment.
   ( ) Deposit from the Buyer in the amount of $ _____has been
      deposited with _____to be applied toward the down payment.
   ( ) An approved copy of your above numbered preliminary title report dated: _____.
   ( )_____.
   ( )_____.
   ( )_____.
   ( )_____.

4. In connection herewith, the following are to be submitted to escrow by the SELLER:
   ( ) Grant Deed to Buyer to be recorded upon close of escrow.
   ( ) An approved copy of your above numbered preliminary title report dated: _____.
   ( )_____.
   ( )_____.
   ( )_____.
   ( )_____.

CONTINUED ON PAGE TWO

- Page One -

5. You are authorized to deliver and/or record all documents and disburse all funds, including the proceeds of any loan deposited herein, when you will issue your current form of _____ policy of title insurance (and Lender's policy as required by Buyer's lender) with liability in the amount of the purchase price or amount of liability required by Buyer's lender, whichever is greater, on the real property described above on Page One.

SHOWING TITLE VESTED IN: _____

_____

SUBJECT TO:

(a) General and special taxes for _____ fiscal year 19 _____ to 19 _____ and subsequent years including reassessments, if any, and including any special district levies or personal property taxes, payment for which are included therein and collected therewith.

(b) Improvement Bonds or Assessments, if any, if assumed by Buyer.

(c) Irrigation District Assessments, if any, paid current at close of escrow.

(d) Covenants, conditions and restrictions, rights of way, easements and reservations of record and in deed to record, if any, and any exception of water, oil, gas, minerals and kindred substances on or under said land now of record or in deed to record.

( ) Deed of Trust □ now of record □ to record, which secures a promissory note in the principal amount of $ _____ payable to _____.

( ) Deed of Trust □ now of record □ to record, which secures a promissory note in the principal amount of $ _____ payable to _____.

6. ( ) You are instructed to obtain a Beneficiary's Statement of Loan Condition on item(s) _____ above, which statement(s) shall be approved by Buyer and Seller prior to close of escrow. Any delinquencies will be paid at close of escrow by □ Buyer □ Seller.

( ) You are instructed not to obtain a Beneficiary's Statement of Loan Condition on item(s) _____ above, and _____ is relieved of any responsibility or liability for the figures used herein which have been supplied by the principals. (See Supplemental Instructions).

( ) Deed(s) of Trust set forth as item(s) _____ above shall be your short form and you are authorized to complete the necessary dates in the note secured thereby.

Any variation in the remaining principal balance of the indebtedness in item(s) _____ above shall be adjusted in _____.

7. Buyer's execution of loan documents shall be deemed approval of the terms and conditions thereof. You are authorized to comply with the Lender's instructions. Buyer and Seller will pay costs in connection therewith as required by lender.

8. Impounds, if any are noticed to escrow holder, are to be □ reimbursed to Seller by Buyer through escrow □ transferred to Buyer without adjustment. Any deficiency in account is to be charged to Seller and paid to lender.

9. Prorate to _____

( ) Taxes based on 19 ____ to 19 ____ tax state-   ( ) Mortgage Insurance Premium.
ment without regard to any reassessments.   ( ) Irrigation District Taxes.
( ) Interest in existing loan(s) on item(s)   ( ) Homeowner's Association Dues.
_____ above. ( ) Interest on Assessments.
( ) Rents based on approved rent statement ( ) Fire Insurance Premium.
handed you in escrow. Any deposits shall be ( ) _____.
credited to Buyer and charged to Seller.   ( ) _____.
( ) _____.   ( ) _____.
                                    ( ) _____.

CONTINUED ON PAGE THREE

- Page Two -

144

10. Fire Insurance
   ( ) Existing policy to be assigned to Buyer, if transferrable and acceptable.
   ( ) Buyer to obtain new insurance, ☐ First year premium to be paid in escrow.
      ☐ paid receipt to be delivered to escrow.

11. All improvement bonds and/or assessments shall be:
   ( ) Paid in full by ☐ Buyer ☐ Seller.
   ( ) Assumed by Buyer; ☐ paid current by ☐ Buyer ☐ Seller.

12. Pest Control Inspection Fee to be paid by ☐ Seller ☐ Buyer
   Repairs, if any, to be paid by ☐ Buyer ☐ Seller
   ( ) Buyer and Seller to approve copies of Pest Control Inspection Report prior to close of escrow.
   ( ) Pest Control Inspection waived.
   ( ) Funds to be held in escrow for completion after close of escrow. (See Supplemental Instructions)

13. Upon close of escrow, you are authorized to deduct from our respective accounts the customary charges attributable to each, including but not limited to the following as indicated below or in accordance with the estimated escrow statement attached hereto and made a part hereof. Prior to close of escrow Buyer will deposit funds in the form of cash or a CASHIER'S CHECK, in the amount necessary to close this escrow.

	SELLER	BUYER
Owner's Title Insurance Policy Premium	$	$
Lender's Title Insurance Policy Premium		
County Transfer Tax		
City Transfer Tax		
Reconveyance Fee		
Document Preparation		
Recording Fees		
Escrow Fee		
Statement Fee		
Change of Record Fee		
Commission to		

14. Time is of the essence of these instructions. If this escrow is not in condition to close by the "Time Limit Date" of _____ 19 ____ and demand for cancellation is received by you from any principal to this escrow after said date, you shall act in accordance with Paragraph 7 of The General Provisions herein. If no demand is made, you will proceed to close this escrow when the principals have complied with the escrow instructions. These instructions may be executed in counterparts, each of which shall be deemed an original regardless of date of execution or delivery and together shall constitute one and the same document.

ANY AMENDMENTS OF OR SUPPLEMENTS TO ANY INSTRUCTIONS AFFECTING THIS ESCROW MUST BE IN WRITING.

15. If any check submitted to escrow is dishonored upon presentment for payment, you are authorized to notify all principals and/or their respective agents of such nonpayment.

You are to be concerned only with the directives specifically set forth in these escrow instructions and amendments thereto, and are not to be concerned or liable for items designated as "memoranda" in these instructions nor with any other agreement or contract between the parties. These instructions are given to _____ to facilitate the close of escrow and are in no way intended to modify or supersede any written or unwritten agreements between the parties, except as specifically set forth herein.

CONTINUED ON PAGE FOUR

- Page Three -

GENERAL PROVISIONS

1. **Deposit of Funds**
   All funds received in this escrow shall be deposited with other escrow funds in a general escrow account or accounts of   , with any state or national bank, and may be transferred to any other such general escrow account or accounts. All disbursements shall be made by check of
   Any commitment made in writing to   by a bank, trust company, insurance company, or savings and loan association to deliver its check or funds into this escrow may, in the sole discretion of
   , be treated as the equivalent of a deposit in this escrow of the amount thereof.

2. **Prorations and Adjustments**
   All prorations and/or adjustments called for in this escrow are to be made on the basis of a thirty (30) day month unless otherwise instructed in writing.
   The phrase "close of escrow" (C.O.E.) as used in this escrow means the date on which documents are recorded and relates only to proration and/or adjustments unless otherwise specified.

3. **Recordation of Instruments**
   Recordation of any instruments delivered through this escrow, if necessary or proper for the issuance of the policy of title insurance called for, is authorized.

4. **Authorization to Furnish Copies**
   You are authorized to furnish copies of these instructions, supplements, amendments, or notices of cancellation and closing statements in this escrow, to the real estate broker(s) and lender(s) named in this escrow.

5. **Authorization to Execute Assignment of Hazard Insurance Policies**
   You are to execute on behalf of the principals hereto, form assignments of interest in any insurance policy (other than title insurance) called for in this escrow forward assignment and policy to the agent requesting that insurer consent to such transfer and/or attach a loss payable clause and/or such other endorsements as may be required, and, forward such policy(s) to the principals entitled thereto.

6. **Personal Property Taxes**
   No examination or insurance as to the amount or payment of personal property taxes is required unless specifically requested.

7. **Right of Cancellation**
   Any principal instructing you to cancel this escrow shall file notice of cancellation in your office, in writing and so state the reason for cancellation. Upon receipt of such request, you shall prepare cancellation instruction for signatures of the principals and shall forward same to the principals. If no written objection is filed with you upon receipt of the mutually agreeable cancellation instructions signed by all principals and after payment of your cancellation charges, you are authorized to comply with such instruction and cancel your escrow. If written objection is filed, you are authorized to hold all money and instruments in this escrow and take no further action until otherwise directed, either by the principals' mutual written instructions, or final order of a court of competent jurisdiction.

8. **Action in Interpleader**
   The principals hereto expressly agree that you, as escrow holder, have the absolute right at your election to file an action in interpleader requiring the principals to answer and litigate their several claims and rights among themselves and you are authorized to deposit with the clerk of the court all documents and funds held in this escrow. In the event such action is filed, the principals jointly and severally agree to pay your cancellation charges and costs, expenses and reasonable attorney's fees which you are required to expend or incur in such interpleader action, the amount thereof to be fixed and judgment therefor to be rendered by the court. Upon the filing of such action, you shall thereupon be fully released and discharged from all obligations to further perform any duties or obligations otherwise imposed by the terms of this escrow.

9. **Termination of Agency Obligation**
   If there is no action taken on this escrow within six (6) months after the "time limit date" as set forth in the escrow instructions or written extension thereof, your agency obligation shall terminate at your option and all documents, monies or other items held by you shall be returned to the parties depositing same.
   In the event of cancellation of this escrow, whether it be at the request of any of the principals or otherwise, the fees and charges due   , including expenditures incurred and/or authorized shall be borne equally by the parties hereto (unless otherwise agreed to specifically).

10. **Conflicting Instructions**
    Upon receipt of any conflicting instructions other than cancellation instructions, you are no longer obligated to take any further action in connection with this escrow until further consistent instructions are received from the principals to this escrow except as provided in Paragraph 7 of these General Provisions.

11. **Usury**
    You are not to be concerned with any question of usury in any loan or encumbrance involved in the processing of this escrow and you are hereby released of any responsibility or liability therefor.

ALL DOCUMENTS, BALANCES AND STATEMENTS DUE THE UNDERSIGNED ARE TO BE MAILED TO THE ADDRESS SHOWN BELOW:

SELLER: _____ ADDRESS _____ TEL. _____

SELLER: _____ ADDRESS _____ TEL. _____

BUYER: _____ ADDRESS _____ TEL. _____

BUYER: _____ ADDRESS _____ TEL. _____

- Page Four -

146

Closing on time is your goal. It is your mission. You have planned everything around the date. The moving company, kids in school, new job, or just figuring out a new route to the old job. A lot depends on the date you close.

And some of it is money: The taxes you pay, the insurance, even new mortgage payments are all prorated (calculated) based on this mythical closing date. Is it impossible to fix a problem if the date slips a bit? No, but why add the financial inconvenience to the other zillion moving hassles already in the hopper? You won't have to if you make yourself a friend, a persistent friend, of the people in the escrow process.

Finally, just before the closing date, do a final walk-through inspection of the home. Make sure everything you're buying is still in the home. Check for any obvious major damage that may have happened since your last visit or the inspection by the professionals. Did that recent rainstorm leave behind any surprises?

- Escrow is that time period when monies and documents are collected before change of ownership.

- Determine the planned closing date as soon as possible.

- Ask for a date that works for your life.

- Stay in touch with everyone pulling together the pieces of the property puzzle to assure closing on time.

- Do one last walk-through just before closing.

HOMEOWNER ASSOCIATIONS AND NEIGHBORHOOD RULES

Dear Mr. Bryant:

I recently purchased a townhouse and learned, after the sale, that I would be required to join and follow the rules of the homeowner's association. Are these neighborhood organizations legal and what happens if I ignore them?

T.P.

L A W   Homeowner associations and rules developed for a particular building or neighborhood are legal and you are agreeing to follow the rules when you purchase the property.

L I F E   Just when you thought you were escaping the clutches of "big brother" in the form of a landlord, you stumble on something called "homeowner's associations" or "conditions, covenants, and restrictions," (CC&Rs). The two are similar in their intrusion into your life, but very different in how you live with them.

First, homeowner's associations. This pretend governing body is most common in condominium complexes, or planned unit developments (PUDs). Basically, these homes are more self-contained or are in fenced residential communities that would like to separate themselves from the rest of the civilized world. Homeowner's associations can be expensive, frustrating, and dominating. But enough about the good points.

A colleague represents an association of homeowners in a mountain community and the bickering between the board of the association and the homeowners is never-ending. The board is usually made up of people with way too much free time, so restrictions are rampant. The way a home looks, which direction it faces, where you can put recreational vehicles or trash cans, how long a visitor can stay without special permission. It can get worse. And the cost for this special treatment can range from $100 to $1000 per month. You also have to be aware that the association fee can and is routinely raised each year. You better know if there are any limits to these raises too. Be afraid, be very afraid.

Second and not quite as bad are the CC&Rs found in many property papers. These rules usually cover things such as the number of pets you can have, height of your TV antenna or placement of a satellite dish. There isn't normally a neighborhood board, but everyone in the neighborhood has signed the same agreement to follow these rules. Check with your neighbors to see if they are aware of any problems. Unless someone makes a stink about a broken rule, CC&Rs often go ignored. Still, you are agreeing to the rules when you buy. So read them carefully and make sure you can live with them if someone decides to raise that stink.

- Determine if there is a homeowner's association where you plan to buy.

- Are there conditions, covenants, and restrictions (CC&Rs)?

- Know how these local rules will effect you after you buy. Talk to neighbors to find out about any problems.

IT'S TITLE TIME!

Dear Michel James Bryant:

We got through all the contracting and negotiating and we had nice people helping us through escrow. But we didn't learn until after the home sale closed that we should have taken title differently. Is it too late?

T.J.

L A W   When a home sale "closes," the title to the property officially changes from the seller to the buyer and is recorded with the local government. Title is the legal manner in which the property is owned and can be changed at anytime, however, it is critical to do it correctly at the time the sale closes.

L I F E   You're sitting at the escrow officer's desk, sweating. Nervous, excited, visions of your new home colliding with images of your new mortgage payment. You've picked up the pen and you're about to sign the papers when you're asked, "How did you want to hold title to this property?" You say something like, "Uuuhhh, what do you think, honey?"

At this point one of two things happens. If you have an attorney, she explains your options and you take the advice you're paying for and a disaster is avoided. If you're flying solo, the non-lawyer escrow person may say, "I'm not supposed to give you legal advice, but . . ." You are then told this person's understanding of the law controlling title to property. Let's be honest. People who deal in property escrows know the various ins and outs of title to property, but if there is a problem down the road, you can't blame the escrow non-lawyer. You are not paying this person to practice law illegally.

There are three main types of property ownership. The first doesn't come up too often so let's get rid of it quick-like. It's called tenancy-by-the-entirety and only works with married people. In fact, it has been virtually replaced by the most common form of title, joint tenancy.

Joint tenancy can be used between any co-owners, married, unmarried, whatever. The only thing you need to know is that joint tenants have "the right of survivorship." If co-owner one croaks, co-owner two automatically gets the other's share of the property. It doesn't matter if the deceased had a will or what it reads. The title papers are legally more powerful. So, in case of joint tenants—the co-owner survivor gets it all, automatically.

Not so with the third option, tenants in common. They have no right of survivorship. Each co-owner shares equally in the property while alive, but when leaving this life, the deceased's share goes to anybody that person leaves it to, usually by will. Harry and Mary own a house as tenants in common. Harry dies. In his will he has given his share of the home to his mother. Now, Mary and her mother-in-law are owners of the home. Perhaps that's exactly what Mary wanted rather than be burdened with owning the entire home herself. Lucky for Mary she now has help.

If you are buying property as a single person, the issue is easier. Just make sure the title includes some statement that you are taking the property as "an unmarried person," "a single person," "as your sole and separate property," something that makes it clear you are not sharing with anyone else.

- Understand the importance of the type of title you want.

- Joint tenants—surviving tenant gets deceased's share of property automatically.

- Tenants in common—deceased's share goes to the person(s) specified in the will.

PROTECTING YOUR TITLE

Dear Legal Edge:

After we bought our home, we learned that one of the title documents, from a previous owner, had been faked. Now we're looking at big legal bills to clear this up. How could we have avoided this?

D.L.

L A W   A title to property will contain all of the names of owners since the property was first registered with the local government. If you do not insure your title when you buy, you may face legal action by someone claiming to own all or part of your property.

L I F E   Title law. It's old, confusing, and makes you long for the days when handing someone a clump of dirt was all that was needed to show change of ownership. Just for fun someday, go down to your local recorder's office and look up the papers on your home or a friend's home. Now that's a hoot! It's your chance to experience what title search companies do all day, every day. Their job, during escrow, is to search the ownership of the property you're buying to make sure nobody with a claim to ownership is hiding in the legal weeds. To make sure nobody has any claim to all or part of the property—especially not anybody whose MO may be to wait until you've spent serious money making improvements which your claim jumper may claim as his own.

To protect your investment, you need title insurance. There are two types. The first is lender's title insurance and it is really there to protect the bank. And bankers normally require it before they will give you money. They're funny that way. The second is called owner's title insurance and protects you from a surprise that might pop up after the property is in your name. If the title search during escrow missed something or a long lost owner claims some interest in the property, title insurance can cover the expense, including attorney's fees, of clearing up the confusion. Both types of title insurance are usually part of "closing costs" that are paid through escrow when the deal is done.

- Ask which title insurance your escrow people use. Call that company.

- Make sure the policy covers all kinds of title claims and pays all costs including attorney's fees.

BOYFRIENDS AND GIRLFRIENDS BUYING HOMES

Dear Legal Edge:
I have a friend who purchased a house with her boyfriend. I didn't think it was the best idea, but she did it anyway. Are there special problems when unmarried couples buy homes?

S.T.

L A W   The rules that help decide property ownership apply most often to married couples and not unmarried singles buying homes.

L I F E   You rent an apartment together, you buy a home together. Married, schmarried, what's the dif? There is a huge difference. When a married couple buys a home or other real property, there are laws that kick in to help decide ownership. Of course, these issues only come up when a couple splits and of course you two won't, but for the other scads of potential former couples, let's continue.

There are nine community property states: Arizona, California, Idaho, Louisiana, Nevada, New Mexico, Texas, Washington, and Wisconsin. The other forty-one and the District of Columbia are called equal distribution states. When a married couple buys a home in either a community property state or equal distribution state, complex rules will decide how the pie is split if the couple splits. The details of these rules would fill another book, but for our purposes here, you don't get the same help as an unmarried couple (guy-girl, girl-girl, guy-guy), buying a home. You've got to help yourself at the time you buy the home to be protected if things don't work out.

It's very simple. Before closing time, make a list of everything each person is contributing to the home purchase including down payment, improvements, taxes, and insurance. Do the math to figure out each person's percentage of contribution to the purchase.

Item	Stacy	Bill
Down Payment	$4000	$3000
Improvements (drapes, etc.)	450	1000
Taxes, Insurance	875	250
Miscellaneous Closing Costs	355	355
Total	$5,680	$4605
Total Costs Purchase	$10,285	
Percentage Contributed	55%	45%

Contribution at Time of Purchase

Now we know that Stacy has a 55 percent interest in the home at the time of purchase and Bill has a 45 percent interest. This example is close to a 50/50 share, but apparently Stacy wants to be precise. Watch out Bill, this may be a sign of things to come.

This whole exercise in math has little to do with the way the couple takes and holds title to the property on their deed. They will still choose either joint tenancy or tenants in common. So, why the brain teaser with the numbers? To have a starting point for whatever happens while living in the home.

The second step to protect an unmarried couple's investments in their home is a monthly log of expenses. In this log you will include any money either person spends on the home, such as mortgage payment, insurance, and improvements. How detailed you get is up to you. If after five years, Stacy and Bill part ways they can easily figure out who gets what share of the home.

Item	Stacy	Bill
Mortgage Payment	$20,000	$28,000
Improvements	4,600	2,200
Taxes, Insurance	3,400	6,000
Miscellaneous Costs	1,110	900
Sub-Total	$29,110	$37,100
Plus Purchase Costs	5,680	4,605
Total Personal Contributions	$34,790	$41,705
Total Home Cost	$76,495	
Percentage Contributed	45%	55%

Contribution While Living in Home
(60 months)

What do we know from this example? Although Stacy contributed the most to get into the home, Bill gradually increased his percentage by making larger contributions while living in the home. The result: Bill will get 55 percent of any profit on the home and Stacy will get 45 percent. The home sells for $100,000 . . . well that would be too easy, but you get the idea. Currently, more and more unmarried couples are buying homes. Until there are specific laws to answer each ownership question, you need to do the work yourself. Start thinking about it now, before you buy. Is it romantic? No, but being practical seldom is.

- Property ownership laws are not designed for unmarried couples.

- List all contributions each person makes to purchase the home.

- Keep monthly records of all expenses paid by each person to calculate ownership percentage.

PLEASE, NOT MORE INSURANCE!

Dear Mr. Bryant:

The bills just keep coming! We got our final closing statement and noticed an item we didn't remember talking to the bank or escrow people about. Mortgage insurance. Enough is enough. Do we have to pay for this?

R.O.

L A W Lenders have a right to require mortgage insurance if your down payment falls below a certain percentage of the home value.

L I F E It's called private mortgage insurance (PMI). Not to be confused with PMS which also shows up each month and makes people a little tense. PMI is an insurance policy that protects your bank or lender if you go belly up on your home loan. Here's how it works. When you buy a home you put money into the purchase as a down payment. If that down payment is less than a certain percentage of your home value (usually 20 percent), the lender charges you for the insurance to protect the loan. If you put $10,000 down on a $100,000 home, or 10 percent, you will be charged for insurance. It's not cheap, either. Figure about $50 to $75 per month on a $100,000 loan.

Purchase Price Value	$100,000
Down Payment	$10,000
Initial Loan Balance	$90,000
Percentage of Equity to Value	10%

Tracking Equity to Avoid Private Mortgage Insurance

Can you avoid PMI? Sort of. Remember, the insurance is based on a comparison of the money owed on the home loan and the value of the home. If all goes well, your home will increase in value over time. You'll also have made small contributions to equity as you pay down the loan. (Most of your early payments on a loan are for interest only.) In other words, the equity (the difference between what you owe and the home value) will increase over time. At some point you will pass the magic 20 percent level and you can ask the lender to drop the PMI requirement from your loan.

Don't expect the lender to jump up and down with excitement when you no longer need PMI. You have to do the work. You will need an appraisal of your home done by a professional appraiser, or proof of realistically comparable home sales in the area. The professional appraiser is best, but that will cost you $150 to $250. Still, it's a deal if you can save that much in your first three months without a PMI premium.

On the following page are a few more numbers. This is just an example. All of us would like to buy a home that gains 20 percent in value over two years, but you can see how monitoring the value and equity of your home and comparing it to the loan amount will tell you when to ask the lender to drop the PMI. There are a number of proposed federal regulations in the works which will require the lender to notify you, the homeowner, when you no longer need to pay for PMI. Not yet though, so you have your assignment.

Appraised Value	*$120,000*
Loan Balance *($1,000 in payments)*	*$89,000*
Percentage of Equity to Value	*34.8%*

Two Years Later . . .

- Expect to pay for private mortgage insurance (PMI) if you put less than 20 percent down on your home.

- Keep track of the difference between your home value and your loan balance to figure out when you no longer need PMI.

11

LIVING AS A HOMEOWNER

L ife will never be the same. You have now taken on the biggest
financial responsibility most people ever face in their lives. It
is also the biggest long-term commitment—a source of tremendous pride, comfort, and sanctuary. Your home, your castle. Now
let's talk about protecting your investment. To do that we will look
at the many adventures you'll find along the road through home
ownership heaven and, occasionally, home ownership hell.

PERMISSION TO USE SOMEONE ELSE'S PROPERTY

Dear Mr. Bryant:
I wonder if you can answer a question about easement rights. What
are they and do these rights have to be on the title?

D.M.

L A W   An easement is the right to use a portion of another
person's property and can be created by will, deed, or by continued
use without objection.

L I F E How would you like someone traipsing across your property, digging up your lawn, or hooking up equipment in your backyard? They don't even have to ask. They have an easement. The most common easement holder is your friendly telephone or electric company. When you bought your home, you were given notice that part of your property could be used by a utility company to bury lines, stash equipment, or simply as a route to get wherever they need to go. You don't remember being told about that? It's in the title and deed papers.

You can give or ask for an easement. If you need to park your RV in the back yard, but the beast is too big to fit between your home and the neighbor's fence, you can ask the property owner living behind you to let you use a strip of his property to get to the backyard. You may be charged for the right or the neighbor may let you do it free. You are getting an easement to park your RV. You can do the same for your neighbor.

Easements attach themselves to the land. If you move, the easement stays with the property and the new owner gets the easement, even if she doesn't plan on using it, unless the easement is limited to a certain time or number of years. The easement right is recorded with the county and when you do that title search we talked about, such easements will pop up, warning a prospective buyer.

An easement can also be created by using someone else's property, without their permission, for a period of time. Dave has a cabin down by the lake. There is a dirt road from the main highway to the cabin but it is not very direct. Dave discovered that he could cut the corner of his neighbor's property and get to the cabin in half the time. For the past five years Dave has been using this shortcut. The neighbor knows Dave is using the shortcut and has often yelled at him to stay off the property, but has not fenced the area to physically stop Dave.

Easement for Dave? Probably. The weird rules require that Dave use the property for a period of time (five to fifteen years depending on the state), and that he do so without permission. Physically stopping Dave would have ended the continual use of the neighbor's property and there would be no easement. Physically stopping Dave might also have resulted in, as they say in Latin, the nosicus brokenicus of the neighbor, but that's another story.

- Easements are routinely granted to utility companies and included in your title or deed when you buy a home.

- You can use your will to give an easement to use property.

- The use of property, even without permission, can create an easement.

INJURIES NEAR YOUR TURF

Dear Mr. Bryant:

I recently purchased a new home and the sidewalk in front of the home is starting to sink on one end and rise on the other. Who is responsible if someone trips and falls?

D.S.

L A W   Generally, the homeowner is responsible only for injuries caused by unsafe conditions on his property, not property maintained by a city, county, or other government entity.

L I F E   The question here is one of "control." It's a fairly safe bet that you control the house, the back yard, the front yard, the garage—those areas you live in and use for daily activities. But a sidewalk in front of your home may not technically be your responsibility. Often, especially in newer residential areas, sidewalks are put in by the city or county and you give them an easement to use part of your property. Check your deed and title documents to see if you've done this. In some situations, the sidewalk is poured on a part of the property that is not officially yours. Just like the street in front of your house is not yours, the sidewalk may not be on your property either.

So, unless you have poured the cement yourself, you have little responsibility for maintaining it. Having said that, let's go beyond the rules and talk about reality. If you notice a problem on property that is so closely connected to your own that it presents a potential danger, don't ignore it. Send a letter to the city or county. Send a letter to your neighbor if it's a dangerous condition on her property. Send a letter to the builder if the construction is relatively new. Your best protection comes from giving notice to those who are more likely responsible than you. That doesn't mean you won't get sued by some stumble-bum who does a nosedive in your petunias, but you can only do so much. You can also mark the dangerous area with red or orange paint.

- You are responsible for dangerous conditions on the property you control.

- Give notice to those who actually control the sidewalk or other area near or next to your property.

- Paint or otherwise mark the dangerous condition.

NOW THE DANGER IS ON YOUR PROPERTY

Dear Legal Edge:
I had a neighbor who told me about getting sued when a salesman fell off his porch. I guess there was a broken or weak railing. How much do I have to do as a homeowner to keep people safe?

B.D.

L A W   A homeowner must warn of, or make safe, any dangerous condition he knows or reasonably should know about.

L I F E   In the past, the law treated people on your property differently depending on their legal status. For example, a guest at your dinner party would be better protected than someone trespassing in your front yard. But the trend these days is to treat everyone the same. And you're much better off if you do.

What do you know about the condition of your home? Is it in good shape? Are there little dangers you've blown off because you know them so well and know how to avoid them? Like that loose board on the back steps, or that piece of carpeting that always sticks up near the front door. If you know of these problems and someone in your home is hurt, the burden is on you.

What about things that aren't so obvious? Do you have to hire an inspector to make sure your home is up to NASA standards of safety? The rule reads that you are responsible for conditions "you reasonably should have known about." Hmmm. You take a shower every day in the same bathroom. Your only bathroom. A guest stays overnight, uses the same shower and falls when he tries to steady himself on the shower door towel bar which comes flying off. Maybe you should have known about the towel bar problem. Maybe you always drip dry and never use a towel or the towel bar. Maybe the overnight friend, a.k.a. "Larry the Load," would do damage to an industrial strength towel bar.

Remember the rule is that you are responsible for those things you should "reasonably" know about that create a dangerous condition. Use your head. In the normal use and travels through your home you will run across actual dangers or those things heading toward actual danger. Don't ignore them. Once identified you must either warn of the danger or fix the problem. Fixing is best because your friends and guests are klutzes and any warning you give will be too little to save them from themselves. The klutz factor always affects who is truly to blame.

- You are responsible for dangerous conditions on your property if you knew of them or should have known of them.

- Once you recognize a problem, you must either warn others of the danger or fix the problem.

- Others on your property are always responsible to care for their own safety.

ANIMALS, ANIMALS, ANIMALS

Dear Legal Edge:

I like animals. It's not a zoo, but my four dogs and three cats can get excited when people visit. I don't want to lock them up since they're normally so friendly. Last week one of my dogs bit a friend. I felt so bad, and now I'm worried about the legal problems. What can I do?

F.K.

L A W   The old rule allowed a pet owner one "bite" before being held responsible. The assumption was that the animal would reform and never attack again. The trend now is to hold the pet owner responsible unless the animal was provoked by the victim.

L I F E   Little Mikey is riding his bike down the street. Two houses up ahead is a big German Shepherd. Mikey likes dogs so he innocently continues his ride down the street where the dog lies in wait. As he passes in front of the dog's house, the animal lunges at Mikey, biting him on the arm. The kid throws his bike on top of the beast and he and the animal run in opposite directions.

Mikey and his mom find the dog and learn that it has never bitten before. In the good old days, that alone would probably get the dog owner off the hook. Not so these days. Courts are holding dog and other pet owners responsible even if the owner had no clue the animal might bite, claw, knock down, or otherwise injure another person. As a pet owner your only real defense is that the victim somehow provoked the attack.

- New laws make pet owners responsible for injuries to others even if the owner had no reason to believe the pet was dangerous.

- A person provoking or angering an animal may share the blame for any injury.

THAT'S NO PET

Dear Legal Edge:

When I lived out in the country I had lots of animals, like horses, pigs, and a few snakes. Now I am moving into a city. I know I can't bring the horses and pigs, but what about the snakes?

Z.K.

L A W   Local ordinances in cities and towns strongly control what type of animal you may have at home and generally limit you to traditional pets.

L I F E   There's nothing like cuddling up with a big ol' snake to make you feel warm and fuzzy. Unfortunately, many cities specifically list lots of "pets" you can't keep within city limits—ferrets, gerbils, boa constrictors, alligators, even some dog breeds, are now being restricted. It is well within the local government's right to limit the pets you keep at home. You can be fined and the animal can be taken from you for breaking the rules.

There may also be neighborhood rules you agreed to when you bought your home. Those rules may limit the number of typical pets like dogs and cats. So, before moving the menagerie to your new digs, you better find out which of your best friends will get to stay.

- Check with city hall or other local government to find out about pet restrictions.

- Review any neighborhood rules you agreed to when you bought your home to see if there are even more pet limitations.

POOLS, TRAMPOLINES, AND OTHER TOYS

Dear Legal Edge:

I'm a thirteen year old. My parents have been thinking about getting a trampoline and are worried about possible legal problems. What can I tell them?

S.Y.

L A W   You are responsible for injuries to those on your property if you promote or organize an activity and through your negligence someone is hurt while engaged in that activity.

L I F E   The joys of childhood. Running, jumping, swimming in the back yard pool, or over at a friend's house. No more. Now, parents have to get legal counsel before erecting that swing set, trampoline, or jungle gym. The thirteen-year-old letter writer is probably the one wanting the trampoline, not his parents, and he's looking for ammunition to make it happen.

Two things to think about before setting up any activity on your property. First, who's going to be using it? If you plan to limit the use to your own family, that limits the likelihood of getting hauled to court after an accident. Normally one family member is not going to sue another family member living in the same home. Problems come up when little Johnny invites neighbor boy Billy to come over for a bounce, swim, or slide. Now, supervision is your problem. You have just become a playground yard monitor. Is the equipment in good condition? Is the area around the equipment as safe as possible? Is the equipment on cement, grass, bark, or sand?

The other potential problem is with those who use the equipment without your permission—usually trespassing children. You have a much greater responsibility for injuries to curious little ones. If you set up a trampoline on the front lawn with no gate or no barrier between the street and the trampoline, you are begging for trouble. If you put the bouncer in the backyard, surrounded by a fence with a locked gate, you've acted reasonably in trying to prevent trespassing children from getting to the trampoline.

- You must be aware of who is going to use the play equipment.

- Allowing those outside the family to play means taking on the responsibility for their safety.

- Don't make it easy for trespassers, especially children, to get to the equipment.

CAN I PLAY NEXT DOOR? CAN I, HUH?

Dear Mr. Bryant:

My nine year old just came running into the house. He's been invited to go swimming at his friend's house. The friend's mom wants me to sign a letter saying I won't sue if my son is hurt. Is this legal?

D.M.

L A W   A parent can agree to give up, or waive, the right to sue, but the specific details of any accident will determine whether the parent has truly given up that right.

L I F E   More parents are doing whatever they can to limit their liability in situations where there is the risk of injury to the children of others. Will it work? That depends upon the answers to two important questions. Does the parent writing or signing the note really understand what they are signing? And what risks are being assumed?

Dear Ms. Flynn:

My son has permission to play at your home with your son Errol.

Sincerely,

Ms. Smith

That's not a very specific letter. Probably not good enough to keep Ms. Smith from holding Ms. Flynn responsible for, let's say an eye injury suffered by her son during a little sword fight. In fact, no permission letter is 100 percent certain to keep one parent from asking a court to hold another parent responsible. It always depends on the facts and circumstances leading up to the injury. Generally, the less specific the letter is about the activity or the feared injury, the less likely a court will hold that letter against the parent whose child has been injured.

Assuming the letter is specific enough, you have to look at the actions of the parents. Let's use the swimming pool situation as an example. One parent writes and signs a letter for her child.

Dear Neighbor:

My son, Johnny, has my permission to swim in your backyard pool, as long as there is adult supervision at all times. Only under those circumstances, will I assume responsibility if there is an accident involving my child.

Sincerely,

Next Door Neighbor

The next day, Johnny is at the neighbor's house for a swim and his friend's parents are right there with the kids. But, the parents are drunk. They don't see a thing when Johnny is thrown into the side of the pool by their son, suffering a broken arm. Would the accident have happened if the "adult supervision" was sober? Has Johnny's mom completely given up her right to hold the neighbor responsible? Probably not. The required "adult supervision" assumes the neighbors have the ability to watch out for the kids.

- A parent can agree to give up the right to sue a neighbor for injuries to that parent's child.

- The permission letter must be specific about the activity and the possible injuries.

- The actual circumstances surrounding any injury will ultimately decide if the neighbor can be blamed.

GO HOME, KIDS

Dear Legal Edge:

Kids in the neighborhood keep using my driveway for rollerblading. I have politely asked them to stop and I have chased them away, but they keep coming back. Would a "No Trespassing" sign help?

C.S.

L A W   Trespassers have no right to use your property, however, if you knew, or should have known, about a dangerous condition on your property, you might be blamed for any injury suffered by the trespasser.

L I F E   Have you thought about using one of those strips of nails they use to stop criminals during police car chases? Only kidding! You need to take some action, though, and the "No Trespassing" sign is a good start. How about a letter to the parents of the little ones? Let mom and dad know that junior is using your property, without permission, as his personal speedway and you are concerned about injury. Your letter will also demand that the parents keep the kid or kids off your property.

Because you can't rely on the parents to act like adults and handle the situation, do more to protect yourself. Check for dangers on the property. That hole at the end of the driveway, the rocks in the yard from last year's landscape project, the large pink flamingoes stabbed into the lawn. Do anything to make your property less dangerous. Finally, take pictures of the little brats being little brats. Good evidence, just in case all else fails.

- Post visible "No Trespassing" signs.

- Send the parents a letter informing them of their children's behavior.

- Make sure your property is safe.

- Take pictures of the kids when they trespass.

IT'S MY PARTY

Dear Legal Edge:

We have a new home and want to invite a few friends over for a party. We have concerns about our responsibility for guests who drink. How do we handle that?

J.K.

L A W   A party host must act reasonably when providing alcohol to guests and may be responsible for injuries to guests or others if the host's actions contributed to the cause of any injury.

L I F E   The simplest answer to this common question is, "no booze." But the fact is, "no booze," can mean "no guests." I'm not judging, I'm not preaching, I'm just facing the social fact that people drink alcohol. If you are serving it at a party on your property, the law says you must do so responsibly.

Dave has a reputation for getting ripped, plowed, even hammered. You invite him to your party knowing this history. You pour Dave a few drinks over the course of the night and when Dave decides to leave, you are faced with a problem. Can you tell whether he should drive? Have you monitored his drinking so closely that you know exactly how much he's had during the evening? Does he walk, talk, and act drunk? What do you do?

Dave is an easy call. You don't let him drive. Simple. That's because you know Dave and his history. The harder decisions come where you don't know a person well enough to figure out when they've had too much. In those situations, the law says, "be reasonable." If you continue to give alcohol to a person obviously intoxicated, you will be responsible for injuries caused by that person. You contributed. If you took that same person's car keys to keep him from driving and he borrowed the car of another guest, that's not likely your problem, unless you knew the guy had borrowed another car. The trend in the law is to make the party host think—and to hold the host responsible for encouraging or failing to prevent an alcohol-related danger to others.

- "No alcohol" is the safest party option.

- In many jurisdictions, the host is responsible for alcohol-related injuries that happen on the host's property.

- You may also share responsibility for injuries off your property that were caused by someone you knew or should have known was intoxicated if you did nothing to prevent the danger.

GARAGE, RUMMAGE, AND YARD SALES

Dear Michel James Bryant:

We have so much junk, each year we have a yard sale. Are there any rules or tips you can give us on protecting our rights when we set up?

M.S.

L A W   When holding a yard sale you are responsible for the condition of the area in which the sale is held and for any representations you make about the things you sell.

L I F E   Isn't it amazing how many people think the junk you want to get rid of is just what they need? Well, you know what they say, "one man's trash is . . . another man's trash, once his wife finds out what he bought at a yard sale."

One yard sale scenario. You've put up the signs and priced all your goods. You've put the advertisement in the local paper. In the ad you said, "No early birds," but there they are at 6:46 a.m. A lady rushes to get that beautiful purple and orange sweater hanging on the line you've draped between trees, trips over junior's toy truck, and hurts her leg. Are you ready for throngs of shoppers?

The area in which the sale is taking place should be as safe as possible. Pick up any rocks, glass, tools, sprinklers, hoses, doggie deposits—anything that could cause injury to one of your guests. These people are not trespassing on your property. You want them there, so the law puts a higher burden on you to make the area safe.

Later that day, a customer finds your old skis and asks, "Hey, ever have any problems with the bindings?" This is a big sale, so you go on and on about how great the skis have performed and how you are only selling them because you need the cash for your mother's medication. You never get to the story about that time the binding came loose and you twisted an ankle.

Selling items at a yard sale is no different than selling a car or your house. If you make a representation to a buyer, that buyer has the right to rely on what you say. If the snow ski buyer gets hurt when the binding breaks, and he learns you had the same trouble but hid that fact, you have a problem. At the very least he can get his money back. It could be worse if he sues you for his injuries.

- Keep the yard sale area clean and safe by removing anything that might trip your customers.

- Don't make promises or representations about the things you sell.

- Don't lie about or hide defects in the things you sell.

TREES AND THE ROOT OF OTHER GROWING TROUBLES

Dear Mr. Bryant:
I'm gonna cut my neighbor's tree branches. They're hanging over my fence blocking the sun. Can I do that?
D.F.

LAW You may trim any growth crossing your property line, but you may be responsible for replacing the tree or plant if it dies.

LIFE Hey, you don't like your neighbor's tree limbs flopping over your back fence. Cut 'em down! Who does he think he is letting his yard grow wild? Okay, settle down. You do have the right to trim back trees or other plant growth that invade your property, but there is a smart way to do it. Talk to the neighbor first. Let him know of the problem and find out if trimming will cause harm to the tree. You see, if you trim off some big old branches and the tree dies, you might have to buy your neighbor a new tree. Maybe the neighbor needs to bring in an expert tree guy to do it right. If so, you save time and hassle and the tree owner picks up the tab.

One other little twist. Even if the tree or plant might die from your trimming, you can go ahead and do it if the tree is a danger to you or your property.

How about tree roots? Those tunneling tentacles can cause lots of damage. The rules are much the same as for branches and limbs. You have to be more careful, though, because cutting roots can seriously affect the life of the tree. Check with the tree owner before taking a whack at trespassing tree roots.

- You have the right to trim tree branches, roots, or plants that cross your property line.

- You may not trim so severely you kill the tree or plant.

- Talk to the neighbor before any trimming.

- You are liable to replace the tree if it dies.

THE FRUIT AND MORE FROM YOUR NEIGHBOR'S TREES

Dear Mr. Bryant:

My next door neighbor has many trees: fruit trees, maple trees, pine trees. My yard is always full of tree debris and rotting fruit. Who has to clean up this mess?

T.W.

L A W   The fruit, leaves, or other fallout from trees is the responsibility of the tree owner, even when it falls on neighboring property.

L I F E   You're walking down the driveway of your home when you are konked on the head by a pine cone from your neighbor's tree, sustaining several lacerations to your face and scalp. If you face fallout from neighbor's trees, talk to the neighbor. See if you can come to some agreement on how to keep the leaves, pine cones, or fruit from piling up in your yard. Maybe a tree trimming is in order. Maybe you can get him to share in the cost of any cleanup. At this point, the system is not too eager to turn these kinds of life annoyances into legal battles. You can bring your case to court, but don't expect any real sympathy from the judge unless safety is an issue. If the problem gets more severe, actually threatening the safety of those on your property, give the neighbor written notice. That allows her the chance to clean things up.

- Debris or fruit falling from a neighbor's trees is the tree owner's responsibility.

- Write a letter to your neighbor warning of the problem and any safety hazard caused by the tree fallout.

WHAT A VIEW . . . I USED TO HAVE

Dear Legal Edge:

I am considering filing suit against my neighbor to try to force removal of a large group of trees blocking my view of the mountains. Can I do that?

L.S.

L A W   The right to a "view" or "light" is usually controlled by an agreement between property owners or a community association.

L I F E   Fights between neighbors over views are becoming more common. Examples are trees that are too tall or a hedge that keeps light out of a favorite room in your house. The problem? There is no absolute right to light, or a view, or open space. You want to get your neighbor to trim the height of a bunch of trees in his yard? You need a contract between you and your neighbor or specific neighborhood rules that give you the right to hold on to your view. No paperwork? You still have an option if you act in time.

Let's say you move into a new home that has a view of the valley below. You don't want to lose that view, but your neighbor has the right to grow trees on his property if he wants. You may have to pay that neighbor to keep him from blocking your view. This sounds nuts to pay for a view that you already have, just to make sure you don't lose it. But it will be cheaper than going to court, hoping a judge agrees with you. Talk to your neighbor about working out a deal before your view disappears. Then get the agreement recorded as an easement with your title and deed documents. That way, if your neighbor sells the home, the new owner will be controlled by the same agreement to keep your view clear.

Sometimes, a community will develop special view rules that all homeowners must agree to when they buy property in the community. No fences can be more than eight feet tall, no trees taller than fifteen feet are allowed. It is this contract you will ask the court to enforce if your view is blocked by a violation of those rules.

- You have no absolute right to a view, light, or open space even though they seem to come with the property.

- Negotiate a deal with your neighbor to make sure your view isn't blocked.

- Check for special local community rules protecting views.

THE RIGHT TO BREATHE EASY

Dear Legal Edge:

Do I have rights to breathe? Cigarette and cigar smoke make me really sick and I'm tired of holding my breath and keeping my doors and windows shut so my neighbors can smoke.

A.B.

L A W   There is no specific rule protecting the air we breathe in our neighborhoods. If an odor becomes severe enough, it can be attacked in court as a nuisance.

L I F E   Fuming factories, garbage dumps, and hog farms. All have been the subject of lawsuits by neighbors trying to clear the air around their homes. However, no court has yet been asked to decide the case of smoking vs. non-smoking neighbors. It could happen. Not so long ago people actually smoked in their offices and restaurants.

No matter what the smells are like, the court looks at one important factor. Who was there first? If you move into a neighborhood with a hog farm down the road, you came to the nuisance. You accepted the smells when you bought your home. The court also balances the social benefit of the activity which is creating the smell with the homeowner's right to enjoy his or her property. For now it is unlikely that a smoking neighbor's habit will rise to the level of "nuisance."

- A smell in the neighborhood must be a legal nuisance to be attacked in court.

- The court favors whoever was in the neighborhood first.

- The public must benefit from the activity being done by the odor producer.

CAN YOU KEEP IT DOWN, PLEASE?

Dear Legal Edge:

Our neighbors are extremely noisy, especially at night and in the early mornings. They even have another family living with them. What can we do?

K.D.

L A W   Local laws or ordinances control noise levels and the time at which neighbors must be quieter.

L I F E   "You kids, turn that noise down!" Don't we all remember when we were on the receiving end of that demand. Oh well, it's a short trip from being annoying to being annoyed.

We all have the right to the quiet enjoyment of our homes. That would be much easier if we lived in the middle of nowhere, but with society being what it is, we are stuck with local laws to help give us the "quiet enjoyment" we need and deserve, even in neighborhoods where we can hear one another flushing toilets.

The rules normally control two things: the decibels, or actual volume of any noise, and the hours that we get to make the noise. Call city hall or the county to find out your specific restrictions, then get high tech. You can borrow or rent a decibelometer (a noise measuring thingy)—and a cheap tape recorder can help capture the mood of a late-evening noisefest. Armed with this info, talk to the offending neighbor, send a letter, or file a formal complaint with city hall or other local government. Last resort: File a nuisance action to keep the neighbor from bringin' in the funk or the noise.

- Find out the legal noise level limits and quiet hours for your neighborhood.

- Talk to your neighbors—quietly.

- Send a letter, file a complaint, or sue for nuisance if talking doesn't help.

DOG GONE!—I WISH

Dear Mr. Bryant:

What can be done with a barking dog? We've called the owners and the police, but still the dog barks. What should we do next?

G.K.

L A W   Most cities, towns, or communities have dog barking ordinances that provide for warnings and fines against pet owners.

L I F E   You've tried the late-night door knock, and the letter, but nothing seems to quiet the barking dog. The neighbors ignore you or claim they have no control. That's not good enough.

Check with city hall. Find the exact local law that controls dog barking and get the poop on the system. Normally, the city will send out a written warning after the first complaint. Next comes a fine. Then a bigger fine. Eventually, the dog owner may have to get rid of the pet. A civil lawsuit can be filed to claim the dog is a legal nuisance—tough to prove, but your neighbor will get a serious message.

- Make a friendly written request that your neighbor silence the dog.

- File a formal complaint with the city and learn about the complaint process in case further action is needed.

- A civil nuisance action may get your neighbor's attention.

MENDING FENCES

Dear Legal Edge:

Whose responsibility is it to fix the fence between me and my neighbor?

P.C.

L A W   If a fence is on the boundary between two pieces of property it is jointly owned by both property owners who are responsible for repairs or replacement.

L I F E   Let's say the fence is looking a little ratty. It needs a new paint job and it's rotting and crumbling. If it weren't for the trees and bushes alongside, it would probably fall down. You approach the issue in a friendly way: "Hey, Mr. Neighbor, how about we get together, fix this fence, and split the cost?" Your friendly neighbor responds, "How about I completely ignore the problem and wait for you to do it yourself without my help?"

That happens. Even though you and your neighbor share the same fence, you may disagree that it needs fixing or even replacement. Now what? Well you can fix the fence on your own, at your own expense and bill the neighbor for his half. Of course, if he refuses, you may be forced to try to collect in small claims court— alway a fun activity. Unless the fence is very expensive, you may just decide to let it go. If you already have a bad relationship with your neighbor, you might choose to go after him, but the more practical and peaceful solution is to do for yourself and forget the neighbor.

What if you and your neighbor agree you need a new fence but he wants to put up a fancy brick wall costing three times what you're willing to pay? Offer to pay for your half of the cost of the fence you want. If the total for the brick wall is $2,400 and the basic fence would cost $800, give your neighbor $400 toward the cost of the brick wall. It's better than nothing, which is what he'll get if you simply refuse to share in the cost of the expensive brick wall. And you can thank your neighbor for the nice new wall, too.

- A boundary fence is owned and to be maintained by both neighbors.

- Try to agree with your neighbor on repair or replacement options.

- If your neighbor voluntarily replaces or fixes a fence without your input, consider it a gift.

YOU'RE ON MY PROPERTY

Dear Legal Edge:

I suspected it for some time, but now I've had a survey done and my neighbor's driveway is three feet onto my property. I don't want to make a big deal over it, but it is my property. If I don't say anything I might be giving it away, right?

B.D.

L A W   Lines legally identifying a landowner's property can be altered, moved, and legally changed to accommodate the needs of the neighboring property owners.

L I F E   Property lines get screwed up all the time. And you might be giving away a portion of your property unless you enforce your ownership rights. The first step is to get a new survey so everybody agrees where the property lines really fall. If the driveway or other structure can be moved (like a fence or row of trees) then you just move the trees or fence to a point within the confirmed property lines. If the trespassing structure is more permanent, like a house, you've got to go to "Plan B." That usually means the overstepping property owner pays the overstepped property owner for the value of the land overstepped. Make sense? If a driveway slops three feet onto a neighbors two acre lot, and can't be moved, the neighbors can negotiate a value to that piece of the property. Some neighbors are nice enough to do it for free, if the land they lose is insignificant.

Whether you end up paying for the extra dirt or getting it free, you need to change the legal record of title, the deed, to reflect the new property lines. You may need new lot plans drawn or modified and that cost is normally paid for by the guy getting the extra land.

- When you have a property line dispute, get a new survey of the land.

- Decide whether the encroaching fence, driveway, or building can be moved.

- Value the land if the structure can't be moved.

- Record the new legal description to protect both land owners.

CONGRATULATIONS! IT'S A NEW BEDROOM

Dear Attorney Bryant:

We want to add a room to our home. We've just started looking into the whole thing and don't know what to expect. Are there certain things to know about hiring a contractor?

R.K.

L A W   Home improvement contractors are controlled by federal, state, and local laws that will decide responsibility for property damage, injury, or other problems relating to the contractor's work and the construction site.

L I F E   A home improvement project or repair is like having a baby, except the timing is less dependable. Even so, let's start at the beginning, the conception of the idea to do a little home improvement. When you need a professional contractor, ask around for recommendations. Friends, co-workers, family. Now meet with the potential contractors to get a feel for the homeowner-contractor relationship. Oh yes, it is a relationship.

Your first series of questions to any contractor will be about licenses, permits, bonding, and insurance. Not every state requires licenses, but a contractor who has taken the time to meet minimal competency for licensing, even if voluntary, is better than the one who just straps on a tool belt. Licensing is so important in some states that the homeowner has no legal responsibility to pay for work done by an unlicensed contractor. On the other hand, a license does not guarantee perfect workmanship. It is just a starting point.

Do you need a permit for the job? You will, in most cases, if the job involves some addition to your home, or if it is a major repair. The city planning or building department will issue the permit for a fee and, although you may think the money is a waste, you are buying a little peace of mind. A permit means that a building inspector will take a look at the construction as it progresses. If there is a legal violation of the building code, your contractor will have to make things right before continuing the project. A permit will also keep your title clean. A major difference between the home as recorded in the title office and the home as remodeled can lead to a snag when you try to sell the property. Most important, any contractor who refuses or stalls when asked about getting permits is not the contractor you want on the project.

The next item to check is the performance bond. This is your best protection against a contractor who flakes out and walks off the job. A performance bond is really an insurance policy that pays another contractor to finish a job the original contractor couldn't, didn't, or wouldn't complete. The cost of the performance bond is usually built into the total contract price of the job. You might decide not to include this type of protection. On smaller home improvements (less than $10,000), you might be okay. But it's up to you to decide the risk you want to take.

Finally, what kind of insurance coverage does the contractor have? Not just professional insurance for any mistakes she makes on the job, but worker's compensation insurance for her crew. If the contractor doesn't have this insurance, and one of the contractor's employees is hurt while working on your home, you could be sued for lost wages and medical expenses. Ask to see the contractor's worker's compensation insurance policy.

- The contractor should be licensed.

- The contractor should take out permits.

- You should get a performance bond.

• The contractor's workers should be insured against on-the-job injury.

HOME IMPROVEMENT PAPERS

Dear Legal Edge:

We know we need a contract with the company doing our home improvement. You hear all the time about construction delays, labor problems, and bad workmanship. What can we do that will keep those problems to a minimum?

S.R.

L A W The agreement you make with a contractor will control materials, labor, construction delays, payment, and warranties for the home improvement work being done.

L I F E Let's say you've found a contractor you like, one with the experience and concern needed to deliver this home improvement project as you expect. Now it's contract time. See the Contractor Agreement sample form on page 183. This sample includes the critical items you want in your contract.

The most important provision is the scope of the work to be done. This is a basic description of the contractor's job. It will include the location of the work, the materials he will provide, and drawings of the project. Flesh out this part of the agreement with a list of special materials needed (like fancy windows or wallpaper) and attach the list as "Exhibit A."

The next contract clause controls the time to complete the work. The contractor will need to estimate how long his work will take, but you need to tell the contractor to give a realistic estimate, not a best-case scenario. Make sure to include a start date that the contractor can stick to. Your life is going to be turned around by the dust, noise, and inconvenience of construction. At the very least, you need to know when to expect the job to begin. If you have a drop-dead completion date (maybe your

CONTRACTOR AGREEMENT

THIS AGREEMENT, is made this date between _____ (Owner) and _____ (Contractor). In consideration of the following terms and general provisions in connection with home improvement or construction to be performed by Contractor at the following location: _____ .

The Contractor and Owner agree as follows:

Scope of Work: The Contractor will provide all of the materials and perform all of the work as shown on Drawings or described in the Specifications attached to this Agreement as Exhibit "A".

Time of Completion: The work to be performed under this Agreement will commence on or before _____, 19/20 _____ and will be substantially completed on or before _____, 19/20 _____. Time is of the essence. Contractor defines "commencement" for purposes of this Agreement to include the following activities:

Price: Owner will pay Contractor for the material and labor to be performed under the Agreement the amount of _____ dollars ($_____), subject to additions or deductions. All additions or deductions must be in writing and signed by both the Owner and Contractor. Any price for any addition or deduction will be reflected in an increase or decrease in the Agreement price.

Payments: Payments of the Agreement price will be made as follows:

General Provisions:

    1.   If payment is not made when due, Contractor may suspend work on the job until all payments due have been made. The failure to make payments for a period longer than _____ days from the due date will be deemed a material breach of this Agreement.

    2.   All work will be completed in a workman-like manner and in compliance with all applicable building codes or other laws.

    3.   Contractor will provide a plan and scale drawing showing the size, shape and construction specifications for home improvements, a description of the work to be done, of the materials and equipment to be used, and the agreed consideration for the work.

    4.   All work will be performed by individuals duly licensed to perform the work.

    5.   Contractor may hire subcontractors to perform the work under this Agreement, as long as Contractor fully pays any subcontractors and remains individually responsible for the completion of the work.

    6.   Contractor will provide Owner with all releases or lien waivers for all work performed or materials provided at the time the next periodic payment becomes due.

    7.   Contractor is adequately insured for injury to its employees and others suffering loss or injury as a result of acts of Contractor or its employees or subcontractors.

    8.   Contractor, at its own expense, will obtain all necessary permits for the work.

    9.   Contractor agrees to remove all debris and leave the premises in broom clean condition.

    10.   All disputes under this Agreement will be resolved in accordance with the rules of the American Arbitration Association.

    11.   Contractor will not be liable for any delay due to circumstances beyond its control, including strikes, casualty or general unavailability of materials.

    12.   Contractor warrants all work for a period of _____ months after completion.

NOTICE TO OWNER: You have the right to require Contractor to have a performance bond.

_____   _____
Contractor   Date   Owner   Date

_____
Contractor License Number

mother-in-law is coming for a visit), get a commitment in writing that the work will be done before that time, including the likelihood of some delays. If the contractor blows the ultimate deadline, you can get him to pay to put up mom in a hotel.

The contract price is next and is very important. But unlike other contracts, the ultimate price is likely to change. The home improvement process is a collection of surprises that you do your best to minimize and anticipate at the contract stage. Often, it's the homeowner who makes a change that effects the cost—such as better doors, or paint, or carpet. Anytime you change the price of the original agreement, you need to have a written change order. Any change order will include the nature of the change and the cost as an addition or reduction to the original contract price. "We're changing the trim color paint to gold leaf, resulting in a $250 addition in cost to the original contract." Both you and the contractor sign the change order.

How about the payments? The number of payments you make triggers these questions. Are you going to pay off the job in four or more payments? If so, federal law gives you the right to rescind or back out of the deal within three business days of signing the contract. The idea is that, because the contractor is not getting all the money up front, he is protecting the total cost of the job by taking an interest in your property—an "interest" as in a lien or claim against your property. This protects the contractor from getting stiffed if you decide not to pay. The trade-off is your right to cancel the contract if you change your mind within three business days.

You will never pay the full amount for any home improvement before the work is completed. The more expensive the improvement job, the more payments you will make. Make sure the final payment is at least 15 percent of the total contract price and don't pay until you are happy with the work and all liens are off the title.

Finally, every home improvement contract will include standard "boiler-plate" legal language often called "general provisions."

Read these general provisions carefully. As you will see in the sample agreement, licensing, permits, insurance, work standards, disputes, delays, and warranties are all covered, to some degree, in the general language of the contract. Make sure the agreement you sign is specific in the areas just covered. If you don't like something, talk with the contractor about a change and then make that change, in writing on the contract, before the agreement is signed.

- The contract should describe the work specifically.

- Your start and completion time deadlines should be in the contract.

- Price and change order rules must be clear.

- Make payments as work progresses. Never pay the total amount before and unless construction has been completed to your satisfaction.

- Know the general provisions of the contract.

BUT, I PAID FOR THE REMODELING ALREADY

Dear Legal Edge:
We just had our kitchen remodeled. The work went well and was finished on time. Two months after we made the final payment to our contractor, we got a notice from the plumbing subcontractor. He put a $3,500 lien on our house! We paid for everything once already. How can he do that?

TJ.

L A W   Every subcontractor and material supplier who contributes to a home improvement project has the opportunity to make a claim against your home to ensure payment for goods or services provided.

L I F E   This is how it happens. Your contractor has agreed with the subcontractors to pay them for their work and for materials used on the job. You have agreed to pay the contractor, assuming he is going to pass along payment to the subcontractors. But the contractor doesn't pass along anything and takes the extra money to enjoy himself in the islands for a week. The subcontractors still want their money so they attack your home to get paid. In some states you will get notice during  the construction that a subcontractor has the right to put a lien on your property if he isn't paid. But sometimes you don't learn about it until the lien is filed. Either way, this lien messes up title to your home and can lead to fun things like foreclosure, so don't take it lightly. In most cases, you will need a lawyer to help figure out where the money went and to keep the subcontractors happy until the problem can be worked out.

So, if you are about to take on the challenge of home improvement, be certain never to make a home improvement payment solely to your contractor. On each and every check you write make sure that you name both the contractor and the subcontractor. That way, the checks can only be cashed if both parties sign them and you can be fairly certain the subcontractors will get paid.

- Ask your contractor about subcontractor lien rules.

- Make payment checks payable to both the contractor and to each subcontractor to protect against contractor fraud.

- Get immediate legal help if you receive notice of a subcontractor lien on your home.

HOW LONG WILL MY HOME IMPROVEMENT LAST?

Dear Mr. Bryant:

Nine months ago we put in a new bathroom. The toilet seal is already leaking and the door on the sink cabinet is loose. Are there any guarantees or warranties when remodeling is done?

L.C.

L A W   Unless you get specific promises from the contractor, your home improvement work will be warrantied only for a limited time.

L I F E   "Yes, Mr. Smith, we do great work. That's our guarantee. We've never had any complaints." While that may sound comforting, it's not good enough to create any real warranty help if you have a problem.

Home improvement: Is it a product? Is it a service? Actually, it's two purchases in one. The best way to protect your purchase of goods and services is to get them in writing in the contract. Ask the contractor how long his work is warrantied. Ask how long the warranty is for the toilet, sink fixtures, or other products that are part of the improvement job. Most appliances will have multiple year warranties and the contractor should give you the manufacturer's paperwork. If you have a problem with a product, such as a bad toilet, it is the manufacturer who may ultimately be responsible. Still, start your complaint process with the contractor.

Don't give up if you've already done your remodeling and it's too late to protect yourself in the contract. There is an "implied warranty" that the contractor's work and products used must be of a certain quality. This is true even without a written promise. Take up the problem with your contractor. Send a letter describing the problem and be prepared to gather evidence and head to small claims court if you get no satisfaction. "Mr. Contractor, the toilet you installed nine months ago leaks. Please arrange to have the problem fixed or I will have another professional do the work and seek reimbursement in the suitable small claims court." Keep it simple.

- Ask the contractor how long his work is warrantied and get any promise in writing.

- Get appliance or product manufacturer warranties.

- Make sure your contractor understands and accepts that an "implied warranty" exists in his work product.

WORKING IN YOUR UNDERWEAR

Dear Mr. Bryant:
I finally have the chance to work out of a home office, but I'm not sure if there are legal rules I need to follow. At first, I will be working through my home as an employee of a big company, then I will be starting my own business. Please point me in the right direction.
F.H.

L A W Your work activities in your own home are limited by local rules like ordinances, zoning and community agreements.

L I F E So, I'm sitting in my underwear, talking to a client on the phone . . . working at home has certain comfort advantages. But, there are some limitations on what you can and can't do as home work. Check your zoning and neighborhood rules. For example, many parents are now running day care out of their homes and most areas limit the number of children to four or five. Any more than that and the home becomes more of a "business" than a home. You may not be able to operate a veterinary hospital out of your home, or build small aircraft, but any other activity that does not disrupt the neighborhood is probably okay. (Also see "Your Home As an Office," on page 77.) There's only one difference between running a home office where you own the home and a home office where you rent the home. You are the landlord when you own the home. That's one less barrier to beginning your home-based business. Just think about the impact on the neighborhood. Little or none is good.

- Check local zoning ordinances for home business limitations.

- Be certain you did not agree to any neighborhood restrictions on home businesses when you bought your home.

- Your home business shouldn't disrupt the neighborhood.

MY NEIGHBOR'S BUSINESS STINKS

Dear Legal Edge:
This neighbor is running a business, out of his home, making underground shelters out of fiberglass. The business puts out a terrible odor. We don't have zoning laws. What can we do?

L.M.

L A W   If you have no zoning or other local rules to control and limit home businesses, nuisance law will decide which businesses can continue to operate.

L I F E   In rural areas and sometimes in communities growing faster in population than in legal sophistication, it will take test cases to decide the fate of a home business. Let's assume that the business stinks, or is too noisy, or creates too much traffic for the neighborhood. All are potential nuisances. As with any nuisance case, the court wants to know who was in the neighborhood first. Then the balancing begins: Business benefit to the community on one side of the scale and the problems the business causes the community on the other. In the fiberglass shelter case, it seems the activity may cause more harm than benefit, but then I'm not the judge deciding the case. And why is anyone still making underground shelters, anyway?

- If there are no zoning or local rules, "nuisance" law will decide if a business can operate out of a home.

- The business must provide a "benefit" more than it harms the neighborhood.

- Work with neighbors both for and against the business before asking the court for help.

REFINANCING, SECOND MORTGAGES, TAXES . . . OH MY!

Dear Legal Edge:

We bought our home years ago and really want to refinance. Are refinancing and getting a second mortgage the same thing? What about taxes and fees?

D.M.

L A W   When you refinance you are acting as both the seller and buyer of your own home and any title, tax, or ownership issues will be handled just as if buying the home the first time.

L I F E   When interest rates drop, homeowners begin to lust for a quick new loan from the bank—not always the best idea.

Do you want a total refinance or second mortgage? In a total refinance, you are paying off your original mortgage or mortgages and starting a new one. With a second mortgage you are taking an additional loan amount secured by a second deed of trust or mortgage and your original mortgage stays put. So, which is better? It depends. How much is the loan rate of your first mortgage? If the rate is already low, a second mortgage will generate some cash without the cost of a total refinance. Remember, any refinancing will cost you percentage "points" on the loan amount, and all the closing costs that go along with the sale and purchase of any home. If you are not going to be in your home for at least three more years, do not refinance.

If your first mortgage is already a decent rate, getting a second mortgage does nothing except increase your monthly payments. It also makes your property legally easier to attack. If you miss a payment on the second mortgage (which is often sold by the original lender to another, possibly less friendly lender), the holder of the second mortgage can foreclose. You are now dealing with one lender on the first mortgage and another lender on the second. Each of them can kick you out of your home for missing payments.

Taxes. Can you deduct the points or loan fees? How about one of those loans where you get 125 percent of the value of your home to pay off credit card bills? Can you deduct all that interest? Loan companies want you to think you can deduct everything connected to your new loan. That way you'll convince your significant other that, "We would be stupid not to refinance." Okay. Maybe you want to turn five-year credit card debt into part of a 15- or 30-year mortgage debt and convince yourself you're better off because the monthly payments are less. You've got more disposable income. But when you try to deduct all the interest, you uncover limitations. You can deduct only the interest on the loan up to the value of the home. If that baseball pitcher lends you $125,000 on your home worth $100,000, you cannot deduct the interest on the extra $25,000. That part of the loan is above the value of the home. Don't be thrown this curve when refinancing to pay off credit cards.

- A refinance is legally the same as selling your own home to yourself.

- A second mortgage gives foreclosure rights to a second lender.

- Your interest deduction is limited on loans higher than your home value.

- Check with an accountant before any refinancing.

12

SELLING YOUR HOME

People sell their homes for many reasons. You want to move on up to something bigger, something better. Mom and Dad just sent the last little one off to college and need something smaller. Dad got downsized and, without two incomes, the couple can't stay in the home. The neighborhood is changing, there is a job transfer, you need to be closer to Junior's school, you're tired of taking care of a big yard, or the yard's too small for the new dog along with that swing set you bought for the grandkids. Every "For Sale" sign has a different story. But the things you need to know, as a home seller, and the rights you need to protect are all the same.

DISCLOSURE—TELL ME WHAT YOU KNOW

Dear Legal Edge:
What disclosure laws do I need to know to sell my home myself? Are they different from the rules for real estate agents?

M.B.

L A W   The seller of a home has a responsibility to disclose any known defects or potential problems that might affect the value of the property.

L I F E   I won't kid you. Selling your own home can be a major pain. You have to follow the same basic laws that apply to a real estate agent when it comes to disclosure of defects and the subtle wording of "Offers," "Counter-offers," and "The Contract." But if you're up to the challenge you can save lots of money or sell your home faster than the competition because you can afford to sell for less when there is no commission taken from home sale proceeds.

People freak out about "disclosure." What if the water heater blows up a month after we sell? Am I responsible? Then the neighbor kids shave the new owner's cat. Did we have to tell them about the brats next door? Easy now. Just use your head and don't hide problems. The buyer has some responsibility to check out the property too, you know. That's why they do inspections. If you didn't know the water heater had a weak valve, it wasn't obviously broken and you didn't hide the problem, you're probably okay. As for the neighbor kids, the mysterious disappearance of your hamster is not necessarily notice of a neighbor child's propensity to shave small domestic animals.

Are you selling your home in the summer so buyers won't learn about the rainwater runoff problem? That's not a good idea. You are responsible to tell the buyer about any potential problem that might affect the value of the property. If you know winter rains run into and collect in the backyard creating a swamp, fess up. Better than hearing about it next winter when a lawsuit is served on you.

Finally, some states make you fill out a very detailed disclosure form. (See the Real Estate Transfer Disclosure Statement sample form on pages 126–127.) The form covers everything from radon to lead paint to asbestos. Check with your local housing authority or building department for the specific rule in your area.

- If you sell your own home, you must disclose defects you know about or should know about.

- Tell the buyer about any problem that may ultimately affect the value of the property.

- Find out if you need to use a detailed disclosure form.

THE REAL ESTATE AGENT'S SECRET WEAPON

Dear Mr. Bryant:

It's like they have this little secret club. How can I compete with a professional realtor without the Multiple Listings? Is it legal to be excluded from this service?

D.N.

L A W   A real estate agent may legally use the association's listing service to help sell a home and may exclude non-association members from access to this association publication.

L I F E   The biggest disadvantage for the self-help home seller is that monopolistic publication called, "The Multiple Listing Service." Only real estate brokers can list or look for property in this big book of homes for sale. All real estate agents use the book to list homes and all real estate agents use the book to find the right home for their clients. So, you, as a FSBOer (For Sale by Owner), are left out in the cold. Don't despair. Many people have sold homes both with and without an agent. How motivated are you to sell?

Open houses sell homes and you need to have them every weekend. Place simple ads in the newspaper, invest in a decent "For Sale" sign for the front yard, and create hand-out sheets that include a picture of the home and the basics about square footage, features, and price. After a long day of looking at home after home after home, a potential buyer won't remember your place from the rest if you don't do a little marketing. The big boys use brochures and slick signs to sell their products, so why not you? Remember not to lie or make promises in the information you give out. You could be creating a warranty that could haunt you.

- If you sell your own home, you do not have access to a real estate agent's Multiple Listing Service.

- Tell the truth in flyers, brochures, or other materials used to advertise your home.

COVER ME—I'M GOING IT ALONE

Dear Legal Edge:

I've seen your tips on selling a home and I think I'm ready to give it a try. What about all the forms and contracts?

G.K.

L A W   The contract needed to sell a home is no different for a private party than for a real estate agent or lawyer.

L I F E   You could write up your home sale on a napkin from Denny's. Use a crayon if you like. It would still be legal if it was specific about the parties, the price, the date, the home, and the conditions of the sale.

Check the local stationery store for real estate forms. Offers, counter-offers, and real estate sales contracts are all available. Compare them with examples included in this book. Once you are comfortable with the type of form you need, fill out the information needed for both seller and buyer. Be specific and don't forget to include a listing of all property, fixtures, or special items being sold with the home. Include any conditions such as buyer financing or dollar limits on repairs.

Now, pay to have an attorney look over the paperwork. This will only cost you a couple hundred bucks and the lawyer can help you pull together everything you need to close the deal. If you use a title company or escrow company, the attorney will help coordinate. If you want to have the attorney prepare deed or title documents, that can also be done. You decide how much or how little help you need. If you feel uncomfortable, get more help. Remember the typical real estate commission on a $100,000 home is $6,000. You can buy a lot of legal review and coaching for lots less than that.

- Check stationery stores, computer software, and local housing associations for home sale contracts.

- Include specific information on any form used.

- Have the completed contract reviewed by a lawyer and get any legal coaching you need to close the deal.

TURNING THE SALE OVER TO AN AGENT

Dear Legal Edge:

I just don't have the time, and I don't want the headaches of selling my own home. What exactly am I looking for in an agent and who pays for the service?

R.C.

L A W　　Most real estate agents are contractually bound to the seller of the home and have a primary duty to look out for the seller's interests. It is the seller who normally pays for the agent's service through a commission on the sale price of the home.

L I F E　　Whatever the reason, there are times when you need to bring in the professional; a real estate agent. By nature and necessity, agents can be pushy. Don't be pushed. There are several points of negotiation in your agent's contract, called a listing agreement. (See the Exclusive Authorization and Right to Sell sample form on pages 198–199.)

There are two types of agents. You are signing up a "listing" agent. The person who lists your home for sale and deals with the offers that pour in. You will also hear about a "selling" agent. This is just another real estate agent who brings in the buyer or offer. The "listing" agent is the one you work with directly.

Don't give your agent forever to sell. They want six months? Give them three with an option for more if you like them. They want 6 percent, offer 4 or 5. The commission percentage is usually split between the listing agent and the selling agent. If the same person lists and sells, that person takes the whole commission. Negotiate. There are plenty of real estate agents. Your power to deal will depend on the quality, location, and price of your home.

Now check out your agent's work. Does he hold open houses? Does she run newspaper ads? Is the home being shown to many prospective buyers? Are you getting offers? Does the agent know your timetable for moving and does the price reflect your need to sell? A good agent will tell you nicely, "Hey, this place is priced too high, pal." Before you sign up, ask about existing market prices, the agent's marketing plan, and the expected time needed to sell.

- Negotiate the length of any listing agreement.
- Negotiate the agent's commission percentage.
- Ask about plans for marketing your home.
- Be certain your agent is living up to promises.

THE PRICE IS RIGHT, I HOPE

Dear Legal Edge:
We've had our house for sale now for six months and no bites. I told my husband it's priced too high. How do we know the price is right?

S.K.

CALIFORNIA
ASSOCIATION
OF REALTORS®

EXCLUSIVE AUTHORIZATION AND RIGHT TO SELL

1. **EXCLUSIVE RIGHT TO SELL:** _____ ("Seller") hereby employs and grants
   _____ ("Broker") the exclusive and irrevocable right,
   commencing on (date) _____ and expiring at 11:59 P.M. on (date) _____ ("Listing Period")
   to sell or exchange the real property in the City of _____, County of _____
   California, described as: _____ ("Property").

2. **TERMS OF SALE:**
   A. **LIST PRICE:** The listing price shall be _____
      _____ $ _____).
   B. **PERSONAL PROPERTY:** The following items of personal property are included in the above price: _____
      _____
      _____
   C. **ADDITIONAL TERMS:** _____
      _____

3. **MULTIPLE LISTING SERVICE:** Information about this listing ☐ will, ☐ will not, be provided to a multiple listing service ("MLS")
   of Broker's selection and all terms of the transaction, including, if applicable, financing will be provided to the MLS for publication,
   dissemination and use by persons and entities on terms approved by the MLS. Seller authorizes Broker to comply with all applicable
   MLS rules.

4. **TITLE:** Seller warrants that Seller and no other persons have title to the Property, except as follows: _____
   _____

5. **COMPENSATION TO BROKER:**
   **Notice: The amount or rate of real estate commissions is not fixed by law. They are set by each Broker
   individually and may be negotiable between Seller and Broker.**
   A. Seller agrees to pay to Broker as compensation for services irrespective of agency relationship(s), either ☐ _____ percent
      of the listing price (or if a sales contract is entered into, of the sales price), or ☐ $ _____
      AND _____ as follows:
      1. If Broker, Seller, cooperating broker, or any other person, produces a buyer(s) who offers to purchase the Property on the
         above price and terms, or on any price and terms acceptable to Seller during the Listing Period, or any extension;
      2. If within _____ calendar days after expiration of the Listing Period or any extension, the Property is sold, conveyed, leased,
         or otherwise transferred to anyone with whom Broker or a cooperating broker has had negotiations, provided that Broker
         gives Seller, prior to or within **5 calendar days** after expiration of the Listing Period or any extension, a written notice with
         the name(s) of the prospective purchaser(s);
      3. If, without Broker's prior written consent, the Property is withdrawn from sale, conveyed, leased, rented, otherwise
         transferred, or made unmarketable by a voluntary act of Seller during the Listing Period, or any extension.
   B. If completion of the sale is prevented by a party to the transaction other than Seller, then compensation due under paragraph
      5A shall be payable only if and when Seller collects damages by suit, settlement, or otherwise, and then in an amount equal to
      the lesser of one-half of the damages recovered or the above compensation, after first deducting title and escrow expenses
      and the expenses of collection, if any.
   C. In addition, Seller agrees to pay: _____
      _____
   D. Broker is authorized to cooperate with other brokers, and divide with other brokers the above compensation in any manner
      acceptable to Broker;
   E. Seller hereby irrevocably assigns to Broker the above compensation from Seller's funds and proceeds in escrow.
   F. Seller warrants that Seller has no obligation to pay compensation to any other broker regarding the transfer of the Property
      except: _____
      _____
      If the Property is sold to anyone listed above during the time Seller is obligated to compensate another broker: (a) Broker is not
      entitled to compensation under this Agreement and (b) Broker is not obligated to represent Seller with respect to such
      transaction.

6. **BROKER'S AND SELLER'S DUTIES:** Broker agrees to exercise reasonable effort and due diligence to achieve the purposes of
   this Agreement, and is authorized to advertise and market the Property in any medium selected by Broker. Seller agrees to consider
   offers presented by Broker, and to act in good faith toward accomplishing the sale of the Property. Seller further agrees, regardless
   of responsibility, to indemnify, defend and hold Broker harmless from all claims, disputes, litigation, judgments and attorney's fees
   arising from any incorrect information supplied by Seller, whether contained in any document, omitted therefrom, or otherwise, or
   from any material facts which Seller knows but fails to disclose.

7. **AGENCY RELATIONSHIPS:** Broker shall act as the agent for Seller in any resulting transaction. Depending upon the
   circumstances, it may be necessary or appropriate for Broker to act as an agent for both Seller and buyer, exchange party, or one
   or more additional parties ("Buyer"). Broker shall, as soon as practicable, disclose to Seller any election to act as a dual agent
   representing both Seller and Buyer. If a Buyer is procured directly by Broker or an associate licensee in Broker's firm, Seller hereby
   consents to Broker acting as a dual agent for Seller and such Buyer. In the event of an exchange, Seller hereby consents to Broker
   collecting compensation from additional parties for services rendered, provided there is disclosure to all parties of such agency and
   compensation. Seller understands that Broker may have or obtain listings on other properties, and that potential buyers may
   consider, make offers on, or purchase through Broker, property the same as or similar to Seller's Property. Seller consents to
   Broker's representation of sellers and buyers of other properties before, during, and after the expiration of this Agreement.

8. **DEPOSIT:** Broker is authorized to accept and hold on Seller's behalf a deposit to be applied toward the sales price.

   Seller and Broker acknowledge receipt of copy of this page, which constitutes Page 1 of _____ Pages.
   Seller's Initials (____) (____)   Broker's Initials (____) (____)

Published and Distributed by:
REAL ESTATE BUSINESS SERVICES, INC.
a subsidiary of the CALIFORNIA ASSOCIATION OF REALTORS®
525 South Virgil Avenue, Los Angeles, California 90020
PRINT DATE

REVISED 10/97

OFFICE USE ONLY
Reviewed by Broker
or Designee _____
Date _____

EXCLUSIVE AUTHORIZATION AND RIGHT TO SELL (A-14 PAGE 1 OF 2)

Property Address: _____

9. **LOCKBOX:**
   A. A lockbox is designed to hold a key to the Property to permit access to the Property by Broker, cooperating brokers, MLS participants, their authorized licensees and representatives, and accompanied prospective buyers.
   B. Broker, cooperating brokers, MLS and Associations/Boards of REALTORS® are **not** insurers against theft, loss, vandalism, or damage attributed to the use of a lockbox. Seller is advised to verify the existence of, or obtain, appropriate insurance through Seller's own insurance broker.
   C. (If checked:) ☐ Seller authorizes Broker to install a lockbox. If Seller does not occupy the Property, Seller shall be responsible for obtaining occupant(s)' written permission for use of a lockbox.
10. **SIGN:** (If checked:) ☐ Seller authorizes Broker to install a FOR SALE/SOLD sign on the Property.
11. **DISPUTE RESOLUTION:**
    A. **MEDIATION:** Seller and Broker agree to mediate any dispute or claim arising between them out of this Agreement, or any resulting transaction, before resorting to arbitration or court action, subject to paragraph 11C below. Mediation fees, if any, shall be divided equally among the parties involved. If any party commences an action based on a dispute or claim to which this paragraph applies, without first attempting to resolve the matter through mediation, then that party shall not be entitled to recover attorney's fees, even if they would otherwise be available to that party in any such action. THIS MEDIATION PROVISION APPLIES WHETHER OR NOT THE ARBITRATION PROVISION IS INITIALED.
    B. **ARBITRATION OF DISPUTES:** Seller and Broker agree that any dispute or claim in Law or equity arising between them regarding the obligation to pay compensation under this Agreement, which is not settled through mediation, shall be decided by neutral, binding arbitration, subject to paragraph 11C below. The arbitrator shall be a retired judge or justice, or an attorney with at least five years of residential real estate experience, unless the parties mutually agree to a different arbitrator, who shall render an award in accordance with substantive California Law. In all other respects, the arbitration shall be conducted in accordance with Part III, Title 9 of the California Code of Civil Procedure. Judgment upon the award of the arbitrator(s) may be entered in any court having jurisdiction. The parties shall have the right to discovery in accordance with Code of Civil Procedure §1283.05.
       "NOTICE: BY INITIALING IN THE SPACE BELOW YOU ARE AGREEING TO HAVE ANY DISPUTE ARISING OUT OF THE MATTERS INCLUDED IN THE 'ARBITRATION OF DISPUTES' PROVISION DECIDED BY NEUTRAL ARBITRATION AS PROVIDED BY CALIFORNIA LAW AND YOU ARE GIVING UP ANY RIGHTS YOU MIGHT POSSESS TO HAVE THE DISPUTE LITIGATED IN A COURT OR JURY TRIAL. BY INITIALING IN THE SPACE BELOW YOU ARE GIVING UP YOUR JUDICIAL RIGHTS TO DISCOVERY AND APPEAL, UNLESS THOSE RIGHTS ARE SPECIFICALLY INCLUDED IN THE 'ARBITRATION OF DISPUTES' PROVISION. IF YOU REFUSE TO SUBMIT TO ARBITRATION AFTER AGREEING TO THIS PROVISION, YOU MAY BE COMPELLED TO ARBITRATE UNDER THE AUTHORITY OF THE CALIFORNIA CODE OF CIVIL PROCEDURE. YOUR AGREEMENT TO THIS ARBITRATION PROVISION IS VOLUNTARY."
       "WE HAVE READ AND UNDERSTAND THE FOREGOING AND AGREE TO SUBMIT DISPUTES ARISING OUT OF THE MATTERS INCLUDED IN THE 'ARBITRATION OF DISPUTES' PROVISION TO NEUTRAL ARBITRATION."   Seller's Initials ____/____   Broker's Initials ____/____
    C. **EXCLUSIONS FROM MEDIATION AND ARBITRATION:** The following matters are excluded from Mediation and Arbitration hereunder: (a) A judicial or non-judicial foreclosure or other action or proceeding to enforce a deed of trust, mortgage, or installment land sale contract as defined in Civil Code §2985; (b) An unlawful detainer action; (c) The filing or enforcement of a mechanic's lien; (d) Any matter which is within the jurisdiction of a probate, small claims, or bankruptcy court; and (e) An action for bodily injury or wrongful death, or for latent or patent defects to which Code of Civil Procedure §337.1 or §337.15 applies. The filing of a court action to enable the recording of a notice of pending action, for order of attachment, receivership, injunction, or other provisional remedies, shall not constitute a violation of the mediation and arbitration provisions.
12. **EQUAL HOUSING OPPORTUNITY:** The Property is offered in compliance with federal, state, and local anti-discrimination laws.
13. **ATTORNEY'S FEES:** In any action, proceeding, or arbitration between Seller and Broker regarding the obligation to pay compensation under this Agreement, the prevailing Seller or Broker shall be entitled to reasonable attorney's fees and costs, except as provided in paragraph 11A.
14. **ADDITIONAL TERMS:** _____
    _____
    _____
15. **ENTIRE CONTRACT:** All prior discussions, negotiations, and agreements between the parties concerning the subject matter of this Agreement are superseded by this Agreement, which constitutes the entire contract and a complete and exclusive expression of their agreement, and may not be contradicted by evidence of any prior agreement or contemporaneous oral agreement. This Agreement and any supplement, addendum or modification, including any photocopy or facsimile, may be executed in counterparts.

Seller warrants that Seller is the owner of the Property or has the authority to execute this contract. Seller acknowledges that Seller has read and understands this Agreement, and has received a copy.

Seller _____ Date _____   Seller _____ Date _____

Address _____   Address _____

City _____ State _____ Zip _____   City _____ State _____ Zip _____

Real Estate Broker (Firm) _____   By (Agent) _____ Date _____

Address _____   Telephone _____

City _____ State _____ Zip _____   Fax _____

Page 2 of _____ Pages.

REVISED 10/97

┌─ OFFICE USE ONLY ─┐
Reviewed by Broker
or Designee _____
Date _____

EQUAL HOUSING OPPORTUNITY

EXCLUSIVE AUTHORIZATION AND RIGHT TO SELL (A-14 PAGE 2 OF 2)

L A W   There is no legal limit to the price you set for the sale of your home.

L I F E   There's no secret formula. Your home is priced right when somebody else offers to pay the price you ask. Your home is worth exactly what the person buying it is willing to pay. As a guideline, check around and find out the actual sale price of homes similar to yours in the area. Ignore the list prices of other homes, they mean nothing more than your list price.

Some sellers are big on getting an appraisal to figure out sales price. But, appraisers usually inflate the value of the home which does nothing but pump up your erroneous belief that your home is more valuable than it really is. The only exception would be a home that is so unique or isolated that there are no comparisons. If that is your situation—if your home is truly exceptional—then go ahead and call the appraiser.

How urgently do you need or want to sell? The more urgent the need, the lower the price has to be. Any home, anywhere, will sell today if the price is low enough. The market will ultimately tell you if you've found the right price. All you can do is pick a starting point and then fine-tune your way down to the selling point. Now you know enough to do that.

- Check sale prices for homes in the area.

- Use an appraiser only if necessary.

- Your need to sell will effect the sale price of your home.

SO, YOU WANT TO BE A BANKER?

Dear Legal Edge:

The housing market where we live is pretty slow. We are thinking about lending the buyer the money or holding the paper on the sale of our home. What do you think?

V.H.

L A W   A home seller who takes back a mortgage on his own property to assist a buyer has the right to foreclose and retake the property if the buyer defaults on the loan.

L I F E   Basically, a homeowner can agree to act as a bank and take a mortgage and deed of trust on the home he is selling. The buyer makes payments to the seller and the seller can foreclose, just like any real banker—if the buyer blows payments. The seller usually acts as a banker if the buyer doesn't have the money, or can't get a lender to give him a loan.

More often, a buyer won't need the seller to finance the major portion of the home purchase, but will want the seller to take a second mortgage for a smaller amount. This is less risky for the seller because the bank or other commercial lender is taking the major part of the loan risk. Let's say the home sells for $100,000. The first mortgage with Bank National is $85,000. You, the seller, "take back" a second mortgage for $15,000 to help the buyer who is short of cash. The buyer is making payments on the first mortgage to Bank National and making smaller payments to you on the second mortgage. You, as the seller, are still protected by the right to foreclose for missed payments, but, worst-case scenario, you only risk $15,000, the amount of your loan. Make sure you record your second mortgage and deed of trust with the county. Your second mortgage will be listed on the property right beneath the bank's mortgage.

Bad credit, not enough down payment, not enough income are all reasons a bank may reject your buyer and all are reasons you should be nervous about becoming a lender.

- A seller taking back a mortgage steps into the shoes of a lender.

- Try to limit your exposure by taking no more than a small second mortgage.

- Record your mortgage deed and be prepared to foreclose if you don't get paid.

THE HOME SELLER'S PERFECT CONTRACT

Dear Mr. Bryant:

Are there special things we can do to make a contract that will favor us as the sellers of the home?

F.K.

L A W   The home sale contract can include penalties, time limits, and conditions to protect the seller from a buyer breaking the agreement.

L I F E   There's a new sign hanging out in front of homes for sale: "Sale Pending." The home isn't "sold." It isn't still "for sale." It's "pending." It means the seller has a buyer and everyone is waiting for all the paperwork and investigation to be wrapped up and the deal closed. It is during this time that much can happen and the seller is usually the one taking the abuse.

Maybe your buyer doesn't qualify for financing. Maybe the inspections turn up unexpected problems. Maybe the buyer's mother-in-law has decided to move in and the home just isn't big enough. Home sale deals fall through and when they do, you wind up scrambling to find another buyer. You won't scramble so much if you add a few things to your contract.

Limit the number of buyer escape conditions. If the buyer doesn't qualify for financing, okay, she gets out of the deal. But limit the time she has to get the money to thirty days. Limit the number of days for all inspections too. Again, if the buyer leans on the inspectors, their jobs will get done sooner. By shortening the time to meet these conditions, your home will spend less time "off the market" if buyer number one falls through.

Don't forget to include a penalty provision in the contract. Normally, the buyer will lose the deposit or "earnest money" upon backing out of the deal without a good reason. Get as large a deposit as you can. The larger the deposit, the more serious the buyer will be and the less likely to bail.

- Limit the number of days the buyer has to get financing.

- Limit the number of days for inspections.

- Get a large deposit and make sure the contract is clear that the deposit will be kept by seller.

THE SALE IS OVER, HOW ABOUT MY RESPONSIBILITY?

Dear Legal Edge:

We sold our home about two months ago. The son of the buyer was hurt on a septic tank pipe in the backyard. Now the buyer is demanding that we pay for medical bills. When does our responsibility end?

D.P.

L A W   In the absence of fraud or an agreed extension of time, the seller's responsibility for events occurring on the property sold normally ends at the time the sale "closes" and the title officially transfers from the seller to the buyer.

L I F E   The question in a case like this always focuses on what the seller knew at the time of the sale. If little Jimmy was hurt when he fell on a septic tank pipe the seller never knew existed, the seller is not likely to be held responsible. If the seller raked a pile of leaves over the pipe hoping it wouldn't be discovered until after the sale, that is deceptive and the law probably will allow the buyer to recover from the seller. Any fraud, lying, deception, or misleading statements can lead to liability after the sale. If the fraud is substantial, the sale can be reversed and the seller will end up back in the home again, secret septic tank pipe and all.

The other way to hold the seller responsible for events after the sale is to specifically include a time extension in the home sale contract. "Seller agrees to remain responsible for the repair of any defect in the septic system for two months from the date of closing." It's a warranty. You'll notice that the promise is limited to repairs, not damages for injuries. In fact, you've warned about the potential for septic system-related problems by offering the warranty and that acts as "notice" of potential injury. It is not suggested that you make such a warranty. Avoid it, if possible. But in the midst of negotiations, things happen, so understand the potential impact of promises you make when you sell your home.

- The seller's responsibility for injuries or repairs normally ends when the sale closes.

- Fraud, deceit, or misrepresentation before the sale can extend the seller's responsibility beyond the closing date.

- The seller can always agree to be responsible for injuries or repairs as part of the sale negotiation.

YOUR HOME SALE PARTNER—UNCLE SAM

Dear Legal Edge:
We got lucky with the sale of our home and made a fairly good profit. How do we avoid or, at least limit, paying taxes on those profits?
M.K.

L A W   If you made a profit on the sale of your home, you will pay taxes unless you can minimize the profit or reinvest it in a new home.

L I F E   If there is one area of tax law in your favor, it is the law affecting home sale profits. However, these rules are confusing and constantly changing, so check with an accountant for the newest details. First, you have to have a profit. That may sound simple, but there are ways to reduce your profit, on paper anyway. You start with the price you paid for the home, then add the cost of improvements to get the base value. For example,

$75,000 for the home plus $10,000 in landscaping and a pool equals $85,000 as your base value. If you sell for $90,000 the actual profit is only $5,000.

The other tax advantage for homeowners is the "roll-over" rule. If you roll any profit into a new home of equal or greater value, you don't have to pay taxes on the profit. The idea is to keep doing this as you get bigger and better homes, then take the one-time tax break the government offers when you reach senior status. This works great unless you buy an expensive house, sell it, and buy a cheaper house.

- You must have a "profit" to pay tax on a home sale.

- You can limit tax by adding cost of improvements to original home cost to determine base value.

- Use the "roll-over" rule to defer tax on home sale profit.

13

WHEN MOVING OR SELLING ISN'T YOUR IDEA

Buy cheap. Sell high. Pocket the big profit on your home and then move on to the next real estate opportunity, right? Great theory; too bad it doesn't always work. Job problems, relationship problems, health problems, and plain old money problems get in the way. Each of these, alone, or in combination with each other, can lead to the loss of your home. It's like getting evicted in a much more painful and potentially permanent way. Bankruptcy, divorce, and foreclosure. But how do you make the best of these bad situations?

ENJOY YOUR NEW HOME, MR. BANKRUPTCY TRUSTEE

Dear Legal Edge:

We can't make it any longer. I lost my job and my husband barely makes enough to keep us eating. What will happen to the house if we file bankruptcy?

G.Z.

L A W   In most cases, your home becomes an asset of the bankruptcy estate, meaning a trustee will decide how to dispose of the home and your other assets in the best interest of all creditors.

L I F E   Filing bankruptcy doesn't necessarily mean you will lose your home. All right, it certainly increases the odds, but let's be positive here. I will assume you haven't missed enough payments yet to get the bank's attention to start foreclosure proceedings (See the Notice of Default sample form on page 213.) I will further assume that you will have legal help making this difficult decision. So, with that in mind, let's hit the basics to get you thinking in the right direction.

You have your choice of "straight bankruptcy," commonly called chapter 7 bankruptcy, where most or all assets are liquidated and creditors paid, or "reorganization," known as chapter 13 bankruptcy. With chapter 7 bankruptcy, you turn over nonexempt assets to the bankruptcy court or trustee. The assets are sold and creditors collect through the court. Without going into detail about exemptions, many basic needs are not attacked in bankruptcy such as: one car, if not too fancy; work tools; furniture to a certain value; clothes; etc. Even part of your home is protected depending on the state. (It's called a "homestead exemption.") The point is, you will make this exempt property the first subject you ask about when consulting an attorney. And because bankruptcy law is complex and constantly changing, you need to talk to an attorney.

With the chapter 13 type of bankruptcy, you reorganize. Instead of attempting to flush your debts down the toilet, you generate a plan to pay back the dough you owe. The plan takes into account your income, expected income, and a payout of much less than you really owe your creditors. You may pay back as little as five or ten cents on the dollar. For example, if you owe $100,000, your plan is to pay back $15,000 over three years. Of course, all plans must be approved by the bankruptcy court.

With these barest of bits of bankruptcy law in mind, let's look at your home. Do you want to keep the home? For some, the home is their center of gravity; they need it to function. For others, it's just a bunch of wood, bricks and sheetrock. To keep the home under either chapter 7 or chapter 13 you have to do one thing: Make the monthly payments you originally promised to make. If you file for chapter 7 bankruptcy you will work with the lender to catch up on your late payments, late interest, and late charges. But you will still make the regular monthly payments as well. If you file for chapter 13 bankruptcy, you may get to work your late payments, interest and charges into "the plan" and pay them back over a few years. But, you will still make the regular monthly payments. It's up to the lender and the bankruptcy court to approve these arrangements.

- Chapter 7 bankruptcy is straight bankruptcy of non-exempt assets.

- Chapter 13 bankruptcy is reorganizing to pay creditors.

- You may get to keep your home even if you file bankruptcy.

- You will still have to pay all late charges or fees in addition to your regular monthly payment.

- Check on the "Homestead Exemption" rules for your area.

D-I-V-O-R-C-E SPELLS "FOR SALE"

Dear Mr. Bryant:
I am going through a divorce and my husband says he doesn't want the house. I have been told I can have him sign a quit claim deed, but he is worried about being held liable under the mortgage. Is that true?

B.S.

L A W   When one spouse keeps the home in a divorce, the spouse giving up all rights to the home usually remains on the mortgage and liable to the lender. This is true even though the spouse keeping the home agrees, in the divorce papers, to take on the mortgage responsibility.

L I F E   This has got to be one of the most difficult, and seemingly unfair, things ever explained to a client—a client giving up all interest in the home once shared with a spouse.

To understand how this works, you have to put yourself in the shoes of the bank or lender. The bank loaned $80,000 to a couple who has about a 50/50 chance of making it together the entire 30-year-life of the loan. The bank needed both signatures and their incomes to qualify them for the loan. Ten years later, the couple divorces. The bank has no control over that, but why would it ever let one spouse off the hook for payments, just because their marriage didn't work out? Simply put, the bank won't.

However, as part of the divorce paperwork (normally the "property settlement agreement"), the spouse keeping the home will agree to make all mortgage payments and release the other spouse from that obligation. That's a deal between the two parting spouses, though. That agreement does not control the bank that still has two signatures on the mortgage. But the deal gives the homeless spouse some protection. If the spouse in the house misses mortgage payments and the bank looks to the other spouse for the dough, the non-house spouse can go after the other party to get his money back.

The real life problem is this: If the spouse with the house is missing mortgage payments, there probably isn't much money for the non-house spouse to get reimbursed. You are better protected if you have the right to force a sale of the home before the bank comes after you or your credit is ruined. Include this phrase in your property settlement papers: "The spouse in the house agrees to sell the home if falling behind more than two payments at any time."

- The spouse leaving the home will give the ex a quit claim or inter-spousal transfer deed.

- Both spouses' names will remain on any mortgages originally in both names.

- Try to get some promise the home can be sold before late payments hurt your finances or credit.

WHEN THE BANK COMES CALLING—FORECLOSURE

Dear Mr. Bryant:

We've missed three payments on our home and just got the foreclosure notice from the bank. Is there any way to fix this or should we start packing?

T.H.

L A W   Once a bank starts foreclosure proceedings the homeowner has a limited time to work with the lender to prevent sale of the home and removal from the property.

L I F E   The actual foreclosure notice doesn't look that frightening. It usually reads, "Important Notice," and you'll see the word "default." (See the Notice of Default sample form on page 213.) Don't be fooled. The foreclosure notice is the most powerful attack that can be made on your home. Unless you follow the specific rules to get out of homeowner hell, you will lose your property.

The foreclosure notice will tell you how long you have to catch up on your late payments, plus any penalties, and the notice will normally give you a dollar figure, the amount needed to make things all better. A time limit of three months is normal, but read the notice carefully to make sure. If you pay the total due, you can keep your home. That's the traditional rescue from foreclosure.

Here's a secret. The bank does not want your home. When was the last time you walked into a bank and started shopping for a new home? "Yes, I'd like to make this deposit and can you show me something in a colonial, three-bedroom duplex?" Most banks or lenders are not interested in being real estate agents. They just want to make their money by lending you money. When you get a foreclosure notice, call the lender immediately. Explain your situation, the reason for being late, and the plan to catch up. Offer to make smaller payments over a short period of time and prove to these guys you can and will make up for late payments. Or you may be able to refinance the whole loan. Make sure you and the bank sign a written contract with any new payment terms.

Perhaps you planned on moving anyway. To do that, you'll need more time than a normal foreclosure allows. Go to the bank, explain your plan to sell, and negotiate the time you think you'll need to sell. Remember, this is not a typical home sale situation. This is an emergency sale to avoid foreclosure and save your credit. It should not take as long as the average home sale in your area. If you work out a six-month deal with the bank and still no sale, work out a further extension of time. At some point though, the bank will have to protect its investment and take your home.

- Do not ignore a "Notice of Foreclosure."

- Check the time limit to catch up any late payments and penalties.

- Contact the lender and negotiate a payment plan or the time needed to sell the home.

YOU CAN'T FORECLOSE—I QUIT

Dear Legal Edge:

The bank has started the foreclosure process. We don't really care if we stay in this home, and selling is tough in this area. What happens if we just walk away? What about our credit?

D.J.

L A W   A lender has the option of accepting your home through voluntary transfer rather than the foreclosure process.

L I F E   Okay, so you got in over your head. Too much home for your income or bad luck on the job or a terrible illness. Should that keep you from ever owning a home again? It could if your home is officially foreclosed. Credit is critical when buying a home and the word "foreclosure" is a black mark that isn't easily erased from your credit report or the minds of potential lenders. So, don't let your home go through the foreclosure process. Give it to the bank.

Is there a name for this generous gesture? It is called deeding the home to the lender in lieu of foreclosure. You're simply signing the house over to the lender. You get no money. The bank gets the home and the deal between you is over. Maybe you've heard this described as "walking away from the mortgage." Your credit might show a late payment or two, but that's a heck of a lot better than foreclosure. This works best when you have little or no equity in the home and absolutely no interest in staying in the home. Consider it your chance to save your credit.

- You can avoid foreclosure by signing your deed and giving the home back to the lender.

- Your credit report will not show a foreclosure.

- You will be giving up any equity you have in the home.

RECORDING REQUESTED BY

AND WHEN RECORDED MAIL TO

NAME

STREET
ADDRESS

CITY
STATE
ZIP

Title Order No._____ T.S. No._____ SPACE ABOVE THIS LINE FOR RECORDER'S USE ___ __

IMPORTANT NOTICE

IF YOUR PROPERTY IS IN FORECLOSURE BECAUSE YOU ARE BEHIND IN YOUR PAYMENTS, IT MAY BE SOLD WITHOUT ANY COURT ACTION, and you may have the legal right to bring your account in good standing by paying all of your past due payments plus permitted costs and expenses within the time permitted by law for reinstatement of your account, which is normally five business days prior to the date set for the sale of your property. No sale date may be set until three months from the date this notice of default may be recorded (which date of recordation appears on this notice).

This amount is $ _____ as of _____ , and will increase until your account becomes current. You may not have to pay the entire unpaid portion of your account, even though full payment was demanded, but you must pay the amount stated above. However, you and your beneficiary or mortgagee may mutually agree in writing prior to the time the notice of sale is posted (which may not be earlier than the end of the three-month period state above) to, among other things, (1) provide additional time in which to cure the default by transfer of the property or otherwise; or (2) establish a schedule of payments in order to cure your default; or both (1) and (2).

Following the expiration of the time period referred to in the first paragraph of this notice, unless the obligation being foreclosed upon or a separate written agreement between you and your creditor permits a longer period, you have only the legal right to stop the sale of your property by paying the entire amount demanded by your creditor.

To find out the amount you must pay, or to arrange for payment to stop the foreclosure, or if your property is in foreclosure for any other reason, contact:

_____
(Name of beneficiary or mortgage)

_____
(Mailing address)   (Telephone)

If you have any questions, you should contact a lawyer or the government agency which may have insured your loan.

Notwithstanding the fact that your property is in foreclosure, you may offer your property for sale, provided the sale is concluded prior to the conclusion of the foreclosure.

Remember, YOU MAY LOSE LEGAL RIGHTS IF YOU DO NOT TAKE PROMPT ACTION.

NOTICE OF DEFAULT
AND ELECTION TO SELL UNDER DEED OF TRUST

That   is Trustee under a Deed of Trust dated
executed by
                                              as Trustor, to secure obligations
in favor of
                                                              as Beneficiary
recorded   as document no.   in Book   Page
of Official Records in the office of the Recorder of   County,
California, describing land therein as shown in Deed of Trust described above, said obligations including
note(s)   for the sum of $

That the beneficial interest under such deed and the obligations secured thereby are owned by the undersigned;
That a breach of, and default in, the obligations for which such deed is security has occurred in that payment
has not been made of:

That by reason thereof, the undersigned, present beneficiary under such deed, has executed and delivered
to said Trustee a written Declaration of Default and Demand for Sale, and has deposited with said Trustee such
deed and all documents evidencing obligations secured thereby, and has declared and does hereby declare
all sums secured thereby immediately due and payable and has elected and does hereby elect to cause the
trust property to be sold to satisfy the obligations secured thereby.

Dated

_____   _____

_____   _____

FORM #945

CONCLUSION—THE END—NO MAS

Home Sweet Home. You choose where to live, with whom to live and under what conditions you will live. Then everything goes straight to hell. But, now you have the guide to lead you back. From the time you first decide to buy, through the ordeals of home ownership, to the moment you sell, there are legal questions and potential problems that need your attention.

When you buy, do the research on the home, the neighborhood, your agent, the escrow people handling the deal, and the local government. The more you know before the purchase, the fewer problems you'll have after you move in. While living in your home, be aware of your responsibilities: people visiting your property, activities you hold on your property, workers you hire to improve your property. And know your rights when dealing with neighborhood problems like noise, the kids next door, and running home businesses. Finally, the home sale. Should you do it yourself? Understand how much work you're in for and the legal requirements that you need to follow even if you get sales help from a professional. If the sale isn't your choice, remember you have rights and options even in bankruptcy, divorce, and foreclosure.

Nothing is more important for you and your family than understanding the law that controls the place you call home. By knowing your rights and any limitations, you'll have the legal edge.

INDEX

air quality, 175
animals, *see* pets
Answer—Unlawful Detainer (sample
　form), 99–100
appeal, 40–42
appraisal, 156, 200
arbitration, 23–25, 114
attorneys, whether to hire, 29–33,
　195, 207

bankruptcy, 206–208
bid, construction, 124
bid, home buying, 136–37
binding arbitration, 23
boundaries, property, 179–80
building a new home, 123–24
buying a new home,
　see home buying

CC&Rs (conditions, covenants, and
　restrictions), 148–49
children trespassing, 168
closing, 142, 147, 152
collection costs, 41
commission, 196–97
community property, 153
Complaint—Unlawful Detainer
　(sample form), 97–98
condominium complexes, 148
construction, 123–24
construction contract, *see* home
　improvement contract
constructive eviction, 101–102
Contractor Agreement
　(sample form), 183–84
contractors, 180–88
court clerks, 31, 35–36, 40
court costs, 35
credit checks, 54–55
crime rate, 102–103, 121

damage to rental property, 83–84,
　110–11
defamation, 115

demand letter, 33–34
deposit
　home buying, 129, 140–41,
　202–203
　rental, *see* security deposits
deposit refund statement, 110
disclosure laws, 122, 124–25, 192–94
disclosure statement, 125–27,
　193–94
discrimination, 50–51, 55
divorce, and home owner-
　ship, 208–10
dog barking ordinances, 177
down payment, 137

earnest money, 140–41, 202
easements, 158–60, 174
encroachment of property lines,
　179–80
equal distribution, 153
escrow, 141–47
Escrow Instructions (sample form),
　143–46
estimate, construction, 124
eviction, 94–105
Exclusive Authorization and
　Right to Sell (sample form),
　198–99

fences, 177–78
filing fees, 35–36
financing, 138–39, 201
fixtures, 129, 137–38
foreclosure, 104–105, 210–13

garage sales, 170–71
garnishment, 41
guests, 64–65, 79–80

hardship waiver, 35
home-based businesses
　renter's right to conduct, 65,
　77–78, 188–89
　neighbors', 189–90

ABOUT THE AUTHOR

Michel James Bryant is a practicing attorney with experience in litigating disputes ranging from construction defects to sexual harassment. His practice currently focuses on employment related issues like whistle blowing and discrimination.

The author created the nationally syndicated news feature "The Legal Edge," four years ago. The television program has been recognized by The Associated Press, The Radio Television News Director's Association, The National Press Club and The National Academy of Television Arts and Sciences in the field of consumer journalism. When not traveling to produce the television segments Michel lives, and annoys others, in Sacramento, California.